THE
GERMAN FIFTH COLUMN
IN
POLAND

By THE POLISH MINISTRY OF INFORMATION

Death faces this Polish policeman who is being pointed out to a Nazi soldier by a member of German minority in Poland, who accuses him of having "murdered" German's brother

Edited by Aleksandra Miesak Rohde

Printed in Great Britain December 1940
Reprinted in the United States 2014 by

Dale Street Books

Home of America's Dreams
Silver Spring, Maryland

FOREWORD

FOR many months after the German invasion of Poland public opinion in Western Europe and America was skeptical of the stories about the part played by the German minority in Poland in preparing and executing this invasion. These stories, which spoke of plots and subversion carried on for years, of espionage and sabotage practised on an enormous scale, of parachutists dressed in civilian clothes, or as priests and women, or even, against all international law, wearing the uniform of the invaded State, certainly far surpassed all experiences of previous wars.

Only when similar methods were used in Norway and Denmark, and later in Belgium, Holland, Luxembourg, and France, were the eyes even of the most blind opened. It was proved beyond all doubt that the events in Poland were only the first manifestations of a great plan, thoroughly worked out by Berlin, embracing not only Europe, but other continents also. Everywhere the German minorities became a fit instrument in the hands of the political and military leaders of the Third Reich, everywhere we come up against these same methods of operation, characterized by deceit, hypocrisy, and the absence of all juridical and moral scruples.

Poland was the first to put up an active resistance to the German might, and also was the first to feel all the effects of this type of German operation. Her experiences have lost none of their relevance for the present day. On the contrary, closer acquaintance with them has become a necessity for all the countries who cherish the preservation of their essential independence.

Nazism, like its predecessor, Prussianism, has so great an attraction for the average German that its enormous influence on German minorities abroad is not in the least surprising.

The conception that Germanism is something which surpasses the bounds of political frontiers has been expressed by the well-known German writer, von Hintze, in the following words:

"The painful lot which, since Versailles, has hung like a black cloud over the nation's horizon, has given rise to a new German ideal. In place of

3

a nation of sixty millions which regarded its political frontiers as identical with its national frontiers (Volkstum) we have today a nation of ninety million Germans joining hearts and hands across the political frontiers in one common task for the good of the nation. For of what significance to a nation are the political frontiers, those lines inscribed by the hazards of history on maps of paper? We are everywhere: in Eastern Europe, in North and South America, in Asia, and in Africa. And this numerical power can and must be a force which as such should mean more than warships and cannon. The appreciation of this phenomenon constitutes a great success which we Germans have achieved in consequence of the last war."

Therefore, if we are to believe this apostle of Pan-Germanism, in 1939 there were some thirty million Germans scattered over the world and benefiting from the hospitality of other States. On the other hand, this new national doctrine proclaims the superiority of this idea of the nation (*Volksgedanke*) to the conception of the State (*Staatsgedanke*). Nevertheless, it is to the Reich that the Germans abroad and the German minorities are to owe at least a minimum of loyalty.

For the nations not menaced by German hegemony this state of things involves the abuses of German propaganda and espionage. But for the States directly menaced by the Reich it involves being laid open to purely destructive factors, such as treason, sabotage, and subversion.

Today abundant proof is forthcoming that the German minority in Poland formed the vanguard of the armies of the Third Reich. This minority was acting under direct orders from the German authorities or by various organizations which carefully concealed their real character.

The *Verein für das Deutschtum im Auslande*, one of the most important organizations for the protection of Germans abroad, always openly aided and stimulated the subversive activities of the German minorities.

Again, the *Auslandsinstitut* of Stuttgart, a pseudoscientific organization, is in reality purely political in its character, and a representative of the Information Bureau of the German War Office (*Nachrichtenstelle des Reichswehrministeriums*) is an official member of its governing body. This Institute is an important centre of the Second

Bureau (German Intelligence Service) which works in conjunction with Germans living abroad.

Subversive activities and conspiracy against the State were the programme and political conception dominating the German minorities during the period preceding the war. The philosophical, juridical, scientific, or quasi-pacifist theories preached by German statesmen were only a facade, behind which this programme and conception were advanced.

The Reich exploited not only these theories, but also the minority clauses imposed upon several States in 1919 (which, however, were not made binding on the Reich), in order to undermine from within almost all the States of interest to Germany. Again and again she charged them with oppressing and ill-treating the German minorities.

Thus, Poland was attacked on these grounds even in the days of the Weimar Republic. After the emergence of the Third Reich, but particularly during the two years preceding the premeditated German aggression of September, 1939, Berlin intensified its anti-Polish campaign. The more violent these attacks became, so the more flagrant grew the subversive activities of the Germans in Poland.

Methodical preparations for this situation can be traced back through all the past twenty years, from 1919 onwards. The German minority had been slowly and steadily won over to subversive ideas, and the dynamic quality of the Nazi movement only gave those ideas a new, realistic basis. By September, 1939, the 765,000 Germans who constituted the German minority in Poland formed the nucleus of an army of spies and conspirators who were only awaiting the Führer's order to march.

The present book provides a survey of these activities based upon a selection of depositions carefully assembled and classified in Paris during the six months from October, 1939, to March, 1940. The purpose of publishing such a compilation is not only to serve historical truth, but also, after the tragic experiences of Poland, to provide a warning. Obviously, from this angle it will interest most of all those countries in which there is a more or less compact German minority. But it will also serve to place on their guard those States which in the present situation are directly menaced by espionage, sabotage, and by German-made "putsches." Recent news from the continent of Europe provides further confirmation that the successes of the German army of aggression have been rendered possible only because of the direct collaboration of accomplices: of German residents, together with troops and marines disguised as tourists, commercial representatives, and merchant sailors.

London,
December 1940

TABLE OF CONTENTS

CHAPTER ONE - INTRODUCTORY SURVEY

Minority Problems in Polish-German Relations

INSPIRED by the general principles of justice and respect for the specific national cultures of all peoples, the authors of the Treaty of Versailles supplemented the treaties with a number of special regulations in the form of Minority Clauses. These clauses were to be binding primarily upon those countries which had regained their independent existence after the Great War of 1914-1918. They were not imposed upon Germany, which, so far as the national minorities issue was concerned,[1] was not bound under the Versailles Treaty by any legal or formal international obligations. On the one hand, Germany was free from all obligations in regard to minorities, despite the fact that within its frontiers, exclusive of Jews, there were some 2 million foreign nationals, of which approximately 1.5 million were Poles. On the other hand, the German minorities living in the "new States" had their rights to national culture guaranteed in the form of the Minority Clauses. But, instead of being in the nature of educative principles for the guidance of the "new States," in the hands of Berlin these Clauses very quickly became a convenient instrument for the gradual disintegration of the political relations which were to have constituted the permanent basis of the Peace Treaty.

At once realizing the possibilities of this instrument, the Germans regarded the question of national minorities as of prime importance even during the peace negotiations. It is of interest to recall that the minorities issue was first raised in the Peace Conference by the Jews. But the Germans made it their own. In its reply to the conditions of peace, the German delegation assured the Allies in its note of May 29, 1919, that the Germans were favourable to the idea of the protection of national minorities.

---

[1] Apart from the Geneva Convention relating to Upper Silesia, finally settled in 1922, and valid only for a period of fifteen years.

"That protection," said the note, *"may perhaps be regulated in the most efficacious manner within the framework of the League of Nations. Nevertheless, Germany considers herself obliged to demand that the peace treaty should contain certain guarantees for those of the German minorities which, as a result of the modification of frontiers, have become subject to foreign sovereignty. These minorities must be given the right to develop their German individuality... In addition, it would be desirable to institute cultural autonomy on the basis of the national census. Germany, for her part, is determined to treat the foreign minorities within her territory in conformity with the same principles."*

In the same note (paragraph headed: Guarantees for those Regions transferred in the East) the German delegation demanded special protection for the German minority in Poland, claiming that this was necessary because of the alleged massacres of Jews in Poland!

Exploiting the Minority Clauses, the Germans launched in the international field, and especially in the League of Nations, a methodical attack upon Poland, accusing her of continually violating these clauses. These persistent attacks were a great hindrance to normal Polish-German relations.

Efforts on Poland's part to improve these relations always met with deliberate opposition from Germany, which endeavoured to keep relations with its neighbour in a state of exacerbation. In the spring of 1933, however, it seemed that Poland's efforts might at last be successful. On January 26, 1934, a Polish-German Declaration was signed which stated, *inter alia,* that the moment had come "to introduce a new phase in the political relations between Germany and Poland by a direct understanding between State and State." It continued: "In no circumstances will they (the two signatory States) proceed to the application of force for the purpose of reaching a decision in such disputes..." "Both Governments are convinced," the text declares, "that the relations between their countries will in this manner develop fruitfully and will lead to the establishment of a neighbourly relationship which will contribute to the well-being not only of both their countries but of the other peoples of Europe as well."[2]

As we have pointed out, Poland made continual efforts from the year 1919 down to the signing of this agreement in 1934 to establish good neighbourly relations with the Reich. The best evidence of this is the fact that she did not even take full advantage of the rights granted her under the Treaty of Versailles with regard to the German minority in Poland. Article 297 (b) of the Treaty reads as follows:

"Subject to any contrary stipulation which may be provided for in the present Treaty, the Allied and Associated Powers reserve the right to retain and liquidate all property, rights and interests belonging, at the date of the coming into force of the present Treaty, to German nationals or the companies controlled by them, within their territories, colonies, possessions and protectorates, including territories ceded to them by the present Treaty.

"The liquidation shall be carried out in accordance with the laws of the Allied or Associated State concerned, and the German owners shall not be able to dispose of such property, rights or interests, nor to subject them to any charge, without the consent of that State.

"German nationals who ipso facto acquire the nationality of an Allied or Associated Power in accordance with the provisions of the present Treaty, will not be considered as German nationals within the meaning of this paragraph."

The Treaty thus authorized Poland to liquidate all the properties which, at the date on which it came into force, belonged to the actual German individuals or groups situated within the territories ceded to Poland by the Reich. This liquidation was to take place in conformity with Polish laws, which, in the terms of par. (c) of Article 297, were also to fix the indemnities to be paid to the owners of the liquidated properties.

Nevertheless, during the succeeding twenty years the liquidation of German properties in Poland was carried out with great moderation and deliberation, in order to mitigate the effects as much as possible. The

---

[2] *Polish White Book* (Hutchinson & Co.), pp. 20-21.

Polish-German Convention concluded at Vienna in 1924 also slowed up the rate of liquidation.

Later, to meet the expressed desire of the German Government, negotiations were opened with a view to setting a time-limit for the liquidation of German properties in Poland. All liquidation operations were effectually suspended during the negotiations, which, after being broken off, finally resulted in the conclusion in 1929 of a Polish-German "Liquidation Convention." By virtue of this agreement a large amount of real estate and numerous enterprises were left in German hands.

Thus, while other States took advantage of Article 297 of the Peace Treaty, Poland, on the contrary, applied the principle of tolerance to the German minority. In fact, on September 1, 1939, the date of the German aggression, many Germans who could have been expropriated still retained their property and enjoyed a privileged position in Poland.

A good proof, that, of Polish liberalism. But Poland went even farther in pursuance of a conciliatory policy towards the Reich. After the joint Declaration of 1934, Poland and the Reich signed a declaration definitely regulating the question of national minorities on both sides of the frontier. She did so in the hope not only of settling an issue which the Germans had exploited for attacks on her, but also of influencing the Reich to treat the Polish minority in Germany in accordance with the liberal principles adopted by the Polish State since 1919 towards its own citizens of German nationality.

On November 5, 1937, the German and Polish Governments issued an identic "Declaration on the subject of the treatment of Minorities." The characteristic preamble to this Declaration read:

"In a friendly exchange of views, the German and Polish Governments have had an opportunity of discussing the position of the German minority in Poland, and the Polish minority in Germany. They are in complete agreement that the treatment of these minorities is a matter of great importance for the further development of friendly, neighbourly relations between Germany and Poland, and that in both countries the well-being of the minority is better protected when it is certain that the same principles will be observed in the other country."

The Declaration proceeded to define these principles in the various spheres of culture, religion, economics, etc. But in conclusion it stated:

"The above principles can in no way affect the duty of the minorities to give complete loyalty to the State to which they belong"[3]

This paragraph of the 1937 Declaration bore the unequivocal implication that if such loyalty were observed on both sides it would lead to the settlement of a problem which, owing to Germany's attitude, had been the cause of continual tension in the relations of the two States. But when Germany signed this Declaration she was not thinking of its observance. The Germans continued with utter ruthlessness to force a Germanization policy in relation to their 1.5 millions of Polish minority subjects. Poland, on the other hand, as was fully evident, never ceased to observe the agreement she had signed. The position of the Germans in Poland, which was already good in every respect, only improved still more. And in these circumstances the German minority became a powerful instrument of espionage and subversive activities, and was enabled to play the role of advance-guard of Hitler's army on September 1, 1939.

The Position of the German Minority in Poland

According to official Polish statistics the number of Germans in Poland at the date of the German aggression did not exceed 765,000. Of this number, which agrees with the estimates of the Germans themselves, and in particular the figures of the German *Sejm und Senats-Büro* (the office of the German Parliamentary group in Poland) the majority, consisting of some 400,000 Germans, inhabited the three western regions of Pomorze, Posnania, and Upper Silesia, all bordering on the Reich. The rest were scattered in more or less homogeneous groups over the whole of Poland. One the largest concentrations of the German urban population in the centre of Poland was at the industrial city of Łódź, lying less than 100 miles from the capital, Warsaw. Among

---

[3] Ibid., p. 40

the scattered rural colonists, the largest agricultural group was in Wolhynia, near the Soviet frontier.

The German citizens of Poland did not exceed 2.4 percent of the total population of the State. But Hitler's steadily growing figures for the German Minority finally reached two millions. Such estimates are as false as those of the alleged victims of the atrocities said to have been committed by Poles in September, 1939, against the "loyal" German minority.[4] In this sphere also the Germans applied their "blitz"— propaganda: in the course of two or three months the number of these alleged victims jumped from 5,800 to 58,000!

The German minority, splendidly organized and methodically directed by Berlin, enjoyed the full protection of the law. The rights of Germans were guaranteed by both the Polish Constitutions: that of 1921 and that of April 1935. Article 5, par. 2 of the latter reads:

"The State assures the citizens the possibility to develop their personal qualities as well as their liberty of conscience, of speech, and association. The limits of these liberties are determined by the interests of the State."

Furthermore:

"The citizens owe allegiance to the State and are expected to fulfil conscientiously the duties that this involves." (Art. 6.)
"The rights of citizens to exercise an influence upon public affairs shall be measured according to the value and merits of their efforts." (Art. 7, par. 1.)
"Neither origin, religion, sex, nor nationality may cause any limitation of these rights." (Art. 7, par. 2.)

Several Articles relating to minorities which were part of the 1921 Constitution were retained in that of 1935. Some of the most important of these are worth quoting:

---

[4] 1 It may be added that whilst Dr. Goebbels' propaganda charged Poland at the beginning of the German occupation with having "murdered" 2,000 Germans in Western Poland, in the following months the figures gradually rose to 5,800, 32,000, 58,000, and in the spring of 1940, even to 65,000!

"All citizens have the right to retain their nationality, to cultivate their language, and to maintain their national peculiarities." (Art. 109, par. 1.)

"Polish citizens belonging to national minorities by religion or by language have, equally with other citizens, the right to found, control, and administer at their own cost any charitable, religious, or social institution, school, or other educational establishment, as well as to make free use of their language and to satisfy the requirements of their religion." (Art. 110.)

"The churches of the religious minorities and all other religious associations recognized by the law shall be governed by their own laws, which the State may not refuse to recognize so long as they contain no illegal provisions.

"The relations between the State and these churches or confessions shall be determined by legislative means after agreement with their legal representatives." (Art. 115.)

The juridical position of the German minority was in obvious contrast to that prevailing in the totalitarian regime of the Third Reich, where the only citizens enjoying full rights, in the real meaning of the phrase, were the Germans themselves. The national minorities in Germany, of which the 1.5 million Poles were the most numerous, found themselves in a State based ideologically upon the principles of National Socialism, which laid down that the State was the central organism of the German Nation, and the expression exclusively of that nation's will. The sole representative of that Will, according to German totalitarian theories, is the National-Socialist Party, subjected absolutely to the Führer. Hitler is the one source of law; he is the executor, the judge, and supreme arbiter of Germany and National Socialism. It is obvious that in such a regime there was no room at all for any separate national group outside the German community. In fact, the National Socialists tolerated the existence of Poles in Germany only temporarily and for purely political reasons. On the other hand, the entire machinery of the single-party German regime was directed to the brutal and ruthless destruction of the Polish element.

The juridical principles obligatory in the Third Reich were diametrically opposed to the liberal principles of the Polish Constitution, and were favourable only to this one object of extermination. For the leading tenet of those principles runs: "That which serves the German Nation is in conformity with German law. Nothing is in conformity with the law which would appear to be prejudicial to that nation's existence." On the other hand, the first tenet of the Polish Constitution of 1935 is: "That the Polish State is the common good of all its citizens, without discrimination on the grounds of religion or national origin."

This constitutional framework, characteristic of a very different regime, ensured the best conditions for the development of the national culture of each national minority, including the Germans. The State intervened only when the activities of a particular minority acquired the obvious features of subversion stimulated from abroad.

The Varied Development of the National Life of the German Minority

In these circumstances the Germans were able to develop their activities with freedom in all spheres of life. The following survey is confined mainly to the chief features of this development in the area of the three German minority regions in Western Poland.

In the sphere of economics, according to 1933 statistics, some 26 percent or about 700,000 hectares of the land in the Posnania region was in German hands, although they represented only 8 percent of the population of this province. Of the land owned by the Germans, about 400,000 hectares came in the category of large estates, while 300,000 were in the hands of smaller holders. In the provinces of Pomorze and Silesia the disproportion was still greater between the percentage of the German population and the amount of land owned by it. Such a state of affairs was the result of a very considerate application by the Polish authorities of the rights she possessed with regard to the liquidation of German properties and under the Agrarian Reforms.

To maintain this state of affairs was one of the principal tasks of the foremost representatives of the German minority. The instructions issued by Berlin had the same end in view, and in addition Germany sent large subsidies for the German farmer element, as well as for the agricultural co-operatives.

The statistics available concerning these co-operative societies are very instructive. According to the 1930 statistics of the Co-operative Union Bank, in the region of Posnania there were 356 Polish co-operatives with 209,232 members, while in the same region the Germans had 434 co-operatives with 28,752 members. These figures reveal the freedom of organization enjoyed by the German minority in the sphere of economic development.

Experience proved that the Germans, taking advantage of the great credits flowing from the Reich, were able to build up their economic life by means of these subsidies. Thus they succeeded in forging the main instrument of national resistance, and also gained a certain influence over that part of the Polish population which was directly or indirectly dependent upon the German co-operatives. It goes without saying that these economic centres constituted an excellent basis for subversive and espionage activities.

A further illustration of the German minority's freedom can be drawn from an entirely different sphere, that of the minority press. The Polish 1933 statistics record that the minority Germans possessed altogether 106 periodicals of different kinds. Of these only 32 existed before 1914, and 15 more appeared during the period 1915 to 1920. Thus, 59 periodicals were started between 1921 and 1931. A number of German periodicals were closed down after the Great War, but these were mainly official and propaganda organs. Of the 106 periodicals in 1933, 34 were political dailies issued by various German groups, 17 were economic and professional, 21 were religious, 9 catered for juveniles, 5 were scientific, and 20 were classed as miscellaneous. These figures demonstrate the favourable conditions which existed for the unhampered development of German activities.

German Schools in Poland.—The last general census of the population of Poland, taken in 1931, showed that there were some 400,000 inhabitants in the German language classification within the areas of the western regions. Taking the proportion of children of school age at 10 percent of the total population, the figure of 40,000 German children of school age is obtained.

In 1933, in the region of Pomorze, the Germans had 50 State and private schools, with 3,682 scholars. In Posnania there were 286 schools with 16,366 scholars, and in Upper Silesia 95 schools with 18,688 scholars. Altogether, in all the western regions there were 431 schools with 38,736 scholars. In addition, the German minority in Poland had 9 State colleges and 21 private colleges, with a total of 4,743 scholars.

In that same year 1933 the Poles in Germany had 64 private schools in the territory of the Reich, with 1,892 scholars, as well as one private college with 240 students. Polish State schools existed only in German Upper Silesia, and these 25 schools were attended by 295 scholars. Yet, according to the estimate of the Polish Union in Germany, the Polish minority numbered about 1,500,000, so that on the 10 percent basis there were some 150,000 children of school age. Of this number, barely 2 percent were able to attend Polish schools.

Further examples of the cultural life of the German minority in Poland can be drawn from other spheres. The German Teachers' Union, the *Landesverband Deutscher Lehrer und Lehrerinnen in Polen*, had some 2,000 members, and published two periodicals, the *Deutsche Schulzeitung in Polen* and *Jugendland.* This little army of teachers was always studying, and it even had its own bookshop, the *Pädagogische Hauptbücherei* in Bydgoszcz. At Dornfeld[5] in the Lwów region existed a German People's University. Other organizations, disposing of considerable funds, were specially concerned with the German libraries. These libraries possessed volumes totalling at least 500,000.

In Posnania the Germans had three permanent theatres, in Pomorze four, and in Upper Silesia one, at which the German theatre from Bytom also gave seasons. This does not include the innumerable amateur theatres. A network of choral societies covered the whole of Poland, and there was a similar network of tourist associations; but above all else mention must be made of the sports clubs, which were merely camouflaged paramilitary organizations.

There was also a number of scientific societies, such as the *Historische Gesellschaft für Posen,* at which Rauschning was professor for

---

[5] This little village of German colonists, hundreds of miles from German territory, kept its name throughout the period of Polish sovereignty.

many years; *Deutscher Naturwissenschaftlicher Verein und Politecnische Gesellschaft* in Poznań, the *Theologische Studiengemeinschaft* in Poznań, the *Deutsche Gesellschaft für Kunst und Wissenschaft* in Bydgoszcz, the *Copernicus-Verein für Wissenschaft und Kunst* in Toruń, and the *Muzeum i Archiwum Niemieckie* in Stanisławów, founded in 1928.

Thus the national life of the German minority had taken on a tremendous scope in all spheres of activity. The Polish authorities intervened only when the provocative character of the conspiracies against the State forced them to do so, and when compelled to take steps by the general indignation which these conspiracies aroused among the Polish community. It is no exaggeration to say that during the past twenty years the Germans in Poland, living in the atmosphere of exceptional tolerance allowed by the State authorities, and supported by subsidies flowing abundantly from the Reich, experienced the golden age of their existence. This golden age ended at the moment of their "incorporation" into the Reich, which involved brutally forcing them into the framework of the totalitarian State system.

Political Organization. —The political life of the German minority was concentrated in two main groups. The first was the *Jungdeutsche Partei*, with former Senator Wiesner at its head, which regarded itself as the corresponding organization in Poland to the German National-Socialist Party of Germany. The second group was composed of more conservative elements, which none the less equally stressed their fidelity to the "National Socialist idea." These elements did not have a homogeneous organization; in the Pomorze and Poznań areas they were organized in the *Deutsche Vereinigung*, in the Silesian area in the *Deutscher Volksblock* and the *Deutsche Partei*, and in the Łódź district in the *Deutscher Volksverband*. They had joint representation in the German Council in Poland (*Rat der Deutschen in Polen*), which was composed of representatives of the organizations named. The chief leader of this group was Senator Hasbach.

Speaking on March 3, 1937, in the Polish Senate, Senator Hasbach declared: "At its last congress in Warsaw the German National Council in Poland, inasmuch as it represents the minority organizations in all parts of the country, defined its position with regard to the latest political events."

Of the great economic organizations the *Westpolnische Landwirtschaftliche Gesellschaft*—in abbreviation: *Welage* (the Western Poland Agricultural Society) was under influence of the "German Council in Poland," while the *Landbund Weichselgau* (the Agricultural Alliance of the Vistula area) was under the influence of the *Jungdeutsche Partei*. The leader of the *Landbund* was Senator Wambeck, who was also a leader of the "Young Germans."

The German Catholics had a separate organization, the *Verband deutscher Katholiken*, whose leader was Senator Pant. There were also a Social Democratic organization and a number of other political and social associations.

The leaders of the German minority always had an effective voice in Parliament, and were granted senatorial mandates. At the last elections held in Poland, in 1938, no representative of the German minority was elected to the Polish Sejm (the Lower Chamber). But the President of Poland nominated two Germans, Hasbach and Wambeck, as Senators. Their anti-State activities were greatly facilitated by the fact that they enjoyed Parliamentary immunity. On the other hand, even in pre-Hitler days the Polish minority in Germany was robbed by fraud of a number of its votes, and later, when the National Socialist one-party organization came into power, the Poles were disfranchised so far as electoral rights were concerned.

Declarations of Loyalty Made by the Leaders of the German Minority in Poland

The declarations made again and again in the Sejm and the Senate by the leaders of the German minority reveal the extent of the cynicism of these conspiratorial enemies of the State. Speaking in the Senate on March 9, 1936, "as a representative of the National Socialist German group," Senator Wiesner solemnly declared:

"Consistently with our philosophy we take the attitude today that the Polish Nation, as master of the country, must decide regarding the

forms of the State, the legislature, and the Constitution, as she alone knows the forms which are adaptable to the national character and to the historic role which the Divine Providence has assigned to Poland in the world. As a German national group, we do not wish to influence the form or the direction taken by the State, and leave these exclusively to the Polish nation. As Germans we seek to preserve our nationality, culture, and conditions of life. We take account of the fact that we can accomplish this work and realize this aim only by acknowledging without reservation the existing legal order, by sincerely cooperating in the building up of a powerful State, and by closely identifying our destiny with that of the country.

"...We desire no privileges, but as a German group in a free country we wish to be respected and appreciated as free citizens. On this condition the State will find us sincere and faithful citizens, ready to collaborate for the future of the State."

On June 24 of the same year, standing at the bar of the Senate, the same Senator Wiesner expressed the view of the German minority on the question of the country's defence:

"As to the arming of the State, we share, as members of this House, the idea that the armed strength of the State must be increased to the maximum effectiveness. The security of the citizens and their possessions depends above all else on the ability of the army to present an effective resistance against all danger. We shall therefore support all motions aiming at increasing the defensive powers of the State."

On March 8, 1937, he attempted to justify the creation of an organization of *Hitler-Jugend* in Poland similar to that which existed in the Reich, and insisted that the Polish State also would benefit by this proposal:

"Our efforts will be directed towards gathering our youth of both sexes into one great organization, which will enable us to make them honest Germans, simultaneously conscious of their obligations as citizens of the Polish Republic."

When in response to these ultra-loyal declarations, the Polish side gave expression to doubts and even accusations of irredentism, the German leaders protested most indignantly. In the Senate on March 12, 1936, Senator Hasbach, who, like Wiesner, was afterwards rewarded by Hitler for his treachery to Poland, exclaimed with emotion:

"In the name of the German population I resolutely repudiate all assertions of German irredentism."

On another occasion, indignant that the Germans in Poland were harassed for using the Hitler salute in greeting, although "the Polish courts had decided that this form of greeting was not a punishable misdemeanour," this same Senator Hasbach declared in the Senate"

"I wish to state emphatically that so long as Polish citizens of German nationality use this form of greeting nothing threatens the State or the Government...We must distrust the clenched fist salute of Communism and Bolshevism. The enemy, gentlemen, is on the left!"

It goes without saying that such declarations did not pass unchallenged from the Polish side. On March 12, 1936, one of the Polish senators from Upper Silesia replied:

"I wish to state that, thanks to Polish tolerance and to concessions unknown, in point of fact, in other countries, and particularly in Germany, the German minority in Poland enjoys the same liberties as its brothers in the Third Reich. Such are the facts of the alleged wrongs done to the Germans in Poland and especially in Upper Silesia. I appeal to the honourable Senator Wiesner to try to obtain from Berlin the same national, religious, and cultural freedom for the Polish minority living in Germany as is granted to the German minority in Poland."

As might be imagined, these appeals remained without effect. None the less, the leaders of the German minority continued their anti-State activities with impunity. Almost to the end they proclaimed their loyalty to the Polish State, even while they were preparing down to the smallest detail the conspiracy which was revealed in all its amazing extent in September, 1939.

In a memorandum presented to the President of the Polish Republic on May 12, 1939, in the name of the German minority, Senator Hasbach and the former Senator Wiesner wrote:

"Permeated with the feeling of responsibility incumbent upon us all as much towards the Polish Republic as towards our own German nationality..."

The leaders of the German minority had created yet another organization which escaped the direct everyday control of the State. This was the German Association in Poland of Citizens of the Reich. This organization was in permanent contact with all the Reich diplomatic and consular posts in Poland, and also linked in one organization all the camouflaged emissaries of the National Socialist Party, the spies and the actual directing staff of the German espionage system in Poland. It was an undisguised outpost of the National Socialist Party, the N.S.D.A.P. The very name of this organization left no doubt as to its true nature, and even its initial letters had a familiar ring. It was called *the National-Sozialistische Deutsche Arbeiter-Bewegung* (N.S.D.A.B.).

In contrast to the foregoing picture was the situation of the 1.5 million of Polish population in Germany, who, from the day the Polish-German frontiers were adjusted, were exposed incessantly, first to the persecution and chicanery of the leaders of the Weimar Republic, and then to the ruthless Hitler regime. Their plight is epitomized in the fact that although there was this Polish minority numbering 1.5 million in Germany, only some 2,000 children attended Polish elementary schools.

In such circumstances, the Polish-German reciprocal agreements intended to regulate the position of the minorities on both sides of the frontier brought genuine benefit only to the Germans in Poland, who were residing in a State which constitutionally guaranteed full rights of citizenship to all nationalities. On the other hand, so far as the Poles in Germany were concerned these agreements were regarded by the Germans as only scraps of paper.

CHAPTER TWO - THE MINORITY GERMANS AS THE REICH'S SPIES AND DIVERSIONIST AGENTS

THE unhampered freedom with which the German minority in Poland was allowed to develop activities in the fields of culture, economics, and politics was exploited by them for organizing anti-Polish espionage, from which Berlin was to profit during the coming war with Poland.

These activities began in the years immediately following the war of 1914-18. Their danger to the State was revealed by the *Deutschtumsbund* trial. The *Deutschtumsbund* was a German minority organization existing mainly in Posnania and Pomorze. The trial established beyond all doubt that its activities were entirely directed by Berlin. Its tasks included the financing of the Germans in Poland from funds contributed by the Reich, the collection of information concerning German-owned property in Poland, a strict control of minority activities, and most of all the fostering among the German minority of the idea of a Great Germany (*Grossdeutschland*) embracing also the lands of her neighbours, and in particular territory which had been "wrested away" from Germany in 1919. The circumstance that this territory had previously been stolen from Poland and that the Versailles Treaty returned it to its true owners had no effect whatever on the German predatory mentality.

The Berlin orders were that the *Deutschtumsbund's* activities were to be developed along constitutional lines, with emphasis upon pseudo-loyalty to the Polish State. The trial completely compromised the organization and its leaders, among others M. Hermann Rauschning and M. Graebe, a Polish citizen who on going to the Reich was promoted to the rank of major in the *Reichswehr*. Moved by a spirit of tolerance, the Polish authorities did not draw the requisite lessons from this incident.

Their attitude was no less lenient in regard to the activities of another organization of the same type, which was working in Upper Silesia. The *Volksbund* trial, which involved a minority leader named Ulitz, who is still active, revealed the methods the Germans were adopting to capture the minds of the Polish children, whom they were attempting to transform into "good Germans." The evidence collected in regard to the *Volksbund* indicated, *inter alia*, that the German teaching staff in the schools was receiving a regular and substantial financial subsidy from the Reich. The trial ended with prison sentences of several years for the school inspector Dudek and his companions. This, however, did not prevent the Germans developing open irredentist Germanizing activity in Upper Silesia, activity which received considerable assistance from German heavy industry working in agreement with Berlin.

The distribution of funds from the Reich was effected through the *Westpolnische Landwirtschaftliche Gesellschaft*, which received finance from Berlin through the intermediary of a Dutch bank. The subsidies thus obtained went to maintain various organizations in the spheres of culture, education, and economics. The local minority organizations could never have carried on their extensive anti-State activities without this financial support from outside.

The tasks assigned to the *Deutschtumsbund* and *Volksbund*, which had been dissolved, were also allotted to the *Deutsche Vereinigung*, formed in 1926, and to other above-mentioned organizations of similar character, which acted in other parts of Poland. These organizations maintained a special office for the German deputies and senators in the Polish Parliament. Its headquarters were at Bydgoszcz, but it had branches in most districts. Behind the cloak of immunity conferred on senators and deputies it was able to carry on very effective work.

When Hitler came to power a new organization, the *Jungdeutsche Partei*, came into being. The head of this young, active, and militant party, founded as an agency of the N.S.D.A.P. in Poland, was Wiesner. Its programme threatened the vital interests of Poland. Its activities quickly covered all the life of the German minority, and the restless spirit of its members brought it into conflict with the *Deutsche Vereinigung* and with other similar organizations, appealing to the older men. But these conflicts were the result more of a difference in temperament than in programme, and, in fact, both organizations were getting ready to play the same role. In March, 1931, the head of the *Deutsche Vereinigung* in Bydgoszcz went to Berlin for the celebration of Hitler's birthday, and made his homage to the Führer, which sufficiently illustrates this minority leader's attitude.

Needless to say, the pro-Reich activities were not confined to the three western provinces of Poland. They developed everywhere where there were members of the German minority. In the southeastern part of Poland, for instance, Pastor Zöckler of Stanisławów was in charge of activities. He was mainly concerned with charitable and religious activities, and devoted himself to higher education. He was regarded with special consideration by Berlin. Some years ago the Institute at Stuttgart published a pamphlet by one Dr. Seeliger dealing with the German element in the southeastern provinces of Poland, in which, the author sought to prove that this element must be maintained at all costs, as it would be of great service in connection with the Ukrainian issue as well as in checkmating the plans of the Polish Government in that area. The Germans of the eastern provinces also were permeated with a spirit of hostility towards Poland. The arrest some time prior to the war of a certain Fräulein Faatz, while she was acting as liaison between the German Consulate in Cracow and the German elements in the Lwów and Stanisławów regions, led to the capture of extensive compromising material. In the Wolhynia area it was the German bank at Luck which held the threads of subversive activities. Even in this region, so far removed from the frontiers of the Reich, the Polish authorities caught Germans in possession of *Arbeitsdienst* (Labour Front) membership cards, issued in Germany. And that organization is only one stage removed from German army service.

All these German minority organizations, scattered throughout Polish territory, were linked up through various intermediaries with a special under-secretariat of State in Berlin, which acted as a department for German affairs abroad. At the head of this department, which was also a branch of the German 2nd Bureau (secret service—*Abwehrabteilung*) was a German named Bohle. Here were centralized all the threads of the subversive and espionage activities to which the whole of the German minority in Poland was harnessed.

The scope of these activities is indicated by the fact that, despite the Polish Government's efforts not to endanger Polish-German good neighbourly relations, during the last few years before the war the Polish courts had to handle some three hundred espionage cases per annum. And during the last six months prior to September, 1939, this figure was almost doubled.

In the Pomorze area M. von Gersdorff was the head of the *Deutsche Vereinigung*. He was the most open of all the leaders of the German espionage. His activities were so unconcealed that they even caused disagreements between the Gestapo at Koenigsberg and the Military Intelligence Service at Berlin.

Some six months before the outbreak of war the Polish secret police came upon the track of espionage activities in which the leading figure was one Baldyga, a criminal who had escaped from Poland to Germany to evade a fifteen-year sentence. After keeping him under observation for some time the German Intelligence Service decided to use him for espionage work in Poland. His capture there led to the discovery of a number of very important elements in German espionage, including the names of German Polish citizens engaged in such activities while following their respective professions. Among others an official of the Polish Military Geographical Institute, a certain Reszka, was arrested. Baldyga's confession threw very interesting light on the specific methods employed in the area of the Polish No.1 District Corps Command and the province of Warsaw by the German Intelligence Service. It came out that in these operations use was made of the so-called wandering German teachers (*Wanderlehrer*), and many of these were arrested in various localities.

Needless to say, these wandering espionage elements were not only in contact with innumerable fixed centres, but also were acting under the orders of Colonel Gerstenberg, the Military Attaché to the German Embassy in Warsaw. He was also occupied with espionage on his own account, employing German elements. Two months before the war one of his aides, a Second Lieutenant of the German Air Force who was also on the diplomatic list, was arrested in the act of photographing military objects. He had operated in the vicinity of Mielec, Sandomierz, Starachowice, and Ostrowiec. Besides a roll of films and a Leica camera, compromising notes regarding objects photographed, as well as remarks of a general nature, were found on him. This officer reported, *inter alia*, that in face of the strongly anti-German feeling among the Poles the war against Poland should be waged with the utmost brutality, in order to smash all possibility of effective resistance from the very beginning. Of course, Colonel Gerstenberg informed the Polish authorities that his assistant had been acting on his own responsibility.

Such characteristic activities as the foregoing were carried on everywhere. The closer drew the moment of conflict, so the more and more open grew the subversive and espionage preparations for the war. German transit traffic across Pomorze was more and more frankly exploited in the interests of German propaganda. Germans travelling across Pomorze increasingly violated the prescribed regulations for transit traffic. There was a considerable growth in the numbers of "tourists," who were sent for the purpose of strengthening the morale of the Germans in Poland and assuring them that the day of "reunion with the Reich" was imminent. Simultaneously excursions made by German youth via Danzig to the Reich to take courses in *Heimatslehre* (elementary training in espionage) increased to mass proportions. Flights from Poland to Germany developed on the same scale. Such flights had two objects. On the one hand they had a certain propaganda value. The fleeing Germans arrived with part of their possessions in the Reich and spread stories of how they had been victimized by the Polish terror, thus helping to create the requisite war spirit in the population. In reality, apart from sporadic breaking of German windows by hot-blooded Polish elements, there was no question of any terrorism whatever. Other flights were organized for the definite purpose of joining the German Army or some paramilitary organization. During the last few weeks before the war thousands of Germans fled from Poland to the Reich.

The ramifications of the German subversive and espionage activities were bound to come to light at various points, so furnishing the Polish authorities with ever-increasing evidence of the treachery of the German minority. A few weeks before the outbreak of war there was an attempt to blow up the railway station at Tarnów. An investigation was made, but without result. At about the same time there was an incident at a frontier post in the region of Piekary, not far from Katowice. The

Polish frontier guard who had examined the identification papers of a group of people crossing into Poland felt suspicious of them, and recalled two of the men for further inquiry. As he was questioning them he was struck on the head with a hard object and fell stunned. When he came round he saw one of the two men pointing a revolver at him. He managed to knock the man's hand away, and the shot struck the assailant himself: The rest of the party took to flight, abandoning various articles as they ran. The one who was killed proved to be a Polish citizen. Among the objects abandoned were pistols of the *Orgesch* type, and Czech *Zbrojowki.* Documents found on the man provided clues which led the police authorities to Piekary, where arrests were made. As one German was being conducted to the inquiry two other Germans attacked the policeman and killed him. Fortunately, one murderer was apprehended by passers-by. This man gave valuable evidence, revealing, *inter alia,* that arms were stored in the church at Piekary and at other places near Kielce. All these secret stores were seized.

The inquiry into this affair resulted in the incrimination of a certain German who had been long suspected by the police. But for some time he evaded arrest. By the merest chance, shortly afterwards, the German Consul at Katowice motored to Bytom (Beuthen), accompanied by a man provided with a German passport. A Polish agent on the frontier recognized this man as the wanted German, and arrested him, despite the Consul's protests.

The documents captured in consequence of all these discoveries proved that the Polish authorities had happened upon a diversionist organization engaged in terroristic activities with high explosives, including the attempt at Tarnów. The inquiry revealed that this outrage had been committed by a minority German agent, who was employed by the Polish State Railways at Nowy Sącz. Further attempts to employ high explosives came to nothing. All the Germans arrested were Polish citizens, and some of them had received special "training" at Oppeln. In the course of the investigation the former Senator Wiesner was incriminated. Feeling that affairs were taking a bad turn he reported to the police authorities and declared that he had nothing whatever to do with the business. But a little later he fled to Germany.

The Polish police came upon further traces of this same organization at Wrzesnia, some weeks before the outbreak of war. They arrested some twenty Germans, finding pistols of the same type as before, several automatic pistols, and also explosive materials, in tins bearing the label of the well-known *Pudliszki* canning factory. All the prisoners made complete confessions, which revealed that these weapons had been supplied by Senator Wambeck who, accompanied by his daughter, had brought them in his car. It is interesting to note that in the previous session of the Senate Wambeck had been nominated a senator by the President of the Republic, and had played the part of a German loyal to Poland, who, because of his loyalty, had grown unpopular among German minority circles with pro-Hitler sympathies.

The police also unearthed a subversive organization at Mala Solna, near Łódź. A telegram was sent from Ostrow in Posnania to Mala Solna, reading: "Mother dead; order wreaths." On the strength of this message a search was made at Mala Solna, and minority Germans were arrested as they were actually assembling. And once more both ordinary and automatic pistols were found on them, as well as the *Pudliszki* cans of explosives, etc. "Order wreaths" had been the signal for them to begin their subversive activities.

In the instructions laying down how the Germans were to behave when war broke out it was emphasized that so long as the German Army was some way off from the locality of the particular subversive group this latter must maintain an ultra-loyal attitude, offering the Polish soldiers food, affording them quarters, etc. Only when the German Army was in the vicinity (between five and twenty kilometres) was diversionist activity to begin.

It is striking that preparations for sabotage and diversionist activities were carried out everywhere in an identical manner and according to a single plan. It was so in Bydgoszcz, and also at Łódź, where, as soon as they had news of the approach of the German troops, the diversionist agents assembled in the forests of Tomaszow and fired on the Polish soldiers. The same thing occurred in Silesia and in many other localities throughout Poland.

The diversionists everywhere distinguished themselves by particular bestiality. A very characteristic incident occurred on the eve of the war. A soldier belonging to the 2nd battalion of the Polish Chasseurs regiment lost his way on the road between Tczew and Danzig, penetrating into Danzig territory. He was shot by a German sentry, and later the Germans handed over his body to the Polish authorities, who ordered an autopsy. The examination revealed filth, straw, and other matter in the man's stomach. The body had been sadistically profaned. This incident was a foretaste of the course the German-Polish struggle would take and of the bestial methods later adopted by the German occupation authorities in Poland, on orders from Berlin.

Nobody in Poland had any illusions as to the nature of all these incidents. The very tolerance of the Polish authorities rendered it easy to follow all the diverse channels of German subversive activity. The more the authorities confined themselves to keeping watch on these various activities, the more impudent became the machinations of the German minority leaders. At the bar of the Senate they went on making their complaints right down to the last moment, appealing to the Constitution, to their "proved" loyalty to the State, without considering, in their effrontery, that every one of their visits to the German Embassy or to any of the German Consulates was diligently noted, and that the Polish authorities were informed of their every trip to Berlin or to Frontier centres of German subversive work. The Polish authorities watched equally closely every prearranged "escape" and the famous "excursions" of the young Germans travelling from Poland to the Reich to take courses of party and military instruction. Complete lists of these trainees were in the possession of every district department of Public Safety as well as every frontier police post. In a word, nobody in Poland had any illusions about the fact that the German minority organizations of all kinds, with such societies as the *Deutsche Vereinigung* and the *Jungdeutsche Partei* at the head, were only branches of the Reich N.S.D.A.P., subordinated to that party's department concerned with Germans abroad.

For the sake of maintaining neighbourly relations with the Reich, Poland had tolerated the hostile activities of its citizens of German nationality for many years. But the view was growing in the country that this state of affairs must be ended. This step would certainly have been taken in 1939, in other words, as soon as the future lines of battle had begun to be clearly defined. For liberalism must end when treason begins. Then Poland would not have been open to the reproach of "intolerance," which German-inspired charge had, unhappily, been so often made against her by other countries, even by France and England, since the end of the Great War. And she would have been able to unmask all the extent of the treason committed against her by her several hundred thousand German minority citizens dominated by the psychology of the Prussian jackboot.

But the sudden invasion of Poland prevented this plan from being realized. And the Germans of the minority were able to occupy positions prepared in advance, and in the struggle which raged over Poland to range themselves openly on the side of the invaders, so contributing enormously to the hastening of Poland's military defeat. The Polish Army, which was not mobilized to the full extent possible, was undoubtedly defeated because of the overwhelming numerical preponderance of the German Armies, by those armies' superiority in tanks and bombing aeroplanes. But there was also the active contribution which the army of spies made to the Germans in this unequal struggle. These Polish citizens of German nationality were active all over the Polish territory, from Puck and Gdynia to Katowice, Czortków, and Zaleszczyki; from Wilno, Pinsk, and Luck to Poznań and Zbąszyń, not excluding the capital, Warsaw, and its vicinity.

Of course, not all the Germans in Poland participated in these subversive activities, but practically all the German organizations, except for certain Catholic and Socialist groups, were dominated by elements with a traitorous attitude to the Polish State.

This treachery was all the easier, since the German colonists scattered over the country were not only organized in various legal societies and bodies, but were to be found in every sphere of social life. The Germans were everywhere: in agriculture, in factories as administrative staff and workers, in all the professions, in foreign-owned enterprises, in commerce and the liberal professions. A foreign-owned enterprise of a formally neutral character often concealed German

33

resources: the huge A.E.G. concern, for instance, or Siemens-Schuckert, or the *I.G. Farbenindustrie* works. In addition the German minority included a numerous teaching staff, and many clergy, both Catholic and Protestant. The organizations of a professional or political nature embraced several hundred thousands of the German minority, certainly some four hundred thousand, and these, established chiefly in the three western regions, constituted a very fine mesh of cells available for conspiratorial espionage and diversionist activities while working within legal bounds.

Through the many German Consulates scattered all over Poland (at Warsaw, Cracow, Poznań, Katowice, Cieszyn, Lwów, Bydgoszcz, Toruń, Gdynia, Danzig) this mesh of cells converged upon a central point, namely, upon the German Embassy at Warsaw. From this centre, where a whole General Staff of advisers and pseudo-officials who were really intelligence service officers and party dignitaries were occupied with the subversive movement and preparation for future diversionist activities, instructions were sent to all parts of Poland by means of the chain of Consulates. The immunity conferred by diplomatic exterritoriality greatly facilitated the Embassy's task of maintaining contact with the local organizations of the minority. The organizers of this widely flung activity were the Councillor to the German Embassy in Warsaw, Dr. Ewald Krümmer, and his colleague, Dr. G. Struwe. All this organized network was placed at the disposition of the German General Staff on September 1, and fulfilled its task without reservation. The opinions of neutral observers can be cited in support of this statement.

The Swiss Divisional Colonel, M. Bircher, a well-known military writer, gave a very interesting lecture some time ago, on the German campaign in Poland, at the *Allgemeine Offiziersgesellschaft* at Zurich. The *Neue Zürcher Zeitung* published a report of this lecture in its issue, No. 346, for March 7, 1940. (Der Feldzug in Polen). *Inter alia* the colonel said:

"One of the main causes of the rapid Polish collapse was the perfection with which the extensive espionage system of the German minority in Poland carried out its function; numerous short-wave transmitters kept the German Army command continually informed."

So that the above judgment considers the subversive activity of the German minority the prime cause (*die erste Ursache*) of the Polish collapse.

On this the Swiss publication *Vaterland,* No. 59, for March 9, 1940, made the following comment:

"In our view, though we are not experts on the subject, Colonel Bircher's opinion signifies that the German minority, in other words the civil population, fought side by side with the German armies from the first day of the struggle, and in consequence, in conformity with the laws of war, its members must be regarded as francs-tireurs, wherever they are captured with arms in hand."

The Germans are slanderously accusing the Poles of murdering a large number of the members of the German minority. As already mentioned, the number "murdered" was first stated to be 2,000, later it suddenly jumped to 58,000, and even 65,000. These figures constitute a growing degree of falsehood in German propaganda.

Today it is no longer necessary to refute these falsehoods. It is sufficient to state that in September, 1939, a certain relatively small number of Germans were shot in execution of sentences of courts martial. Those sentenced to death were not "innocent members of the German minority," as the official Nazi propaganda thesis would have it. They were spies, sabotageurs, and diversionists, caught red-handed.

It has to be added that the German authorities in Poland, against all the fundamental principles of international law, are shooting and murdering those Poles who in September, 1939, did their duty to their own country, by pointing out the German spies and diversionists to the Polish authorities or conducting them to the Polish military authorities.

The foregoing Swiss opinion was by no means an isolated instance.[6]

Thus the Polish soldiers had to fight against the invader not only on the battle-front. Wherever Germans were to be found, whether in the west or the east, whether in large or small numbers, they fired at the

---

[6] Even the semi-official Italian *Popolo di Roma* of April 10, 1940, stresses that the military defeat of the Polish Army was contributed to by the activities of the German minority, co-operating with Gestapo agents and the German espionage. It would be difficult to find a more convincing testimony!

Polish soldiers at night, they burned down the buildings in which the troops were quartered, they cut the telephone wires. Often disguised as Polish soldiers or even as officers, the trouble-makers attacked and disorganized the rear. They signalled details of Polish dispositions with the aid of coloured rockets. They ambushed the Polish troops, and frequently mixed mustard-gas in the water they provided for washing purposes.

If there were but two houses occupied by Germans in any village, there was invariably at least one man capable of diversionist activities, and not merely of a sporadic nature, for he was fully prepared, armed, and acquainted with the password used by his kind.

The German armies which invaded Poland were furnished with the requisite instructions concerning the possibility of utilizing the German minority and of recognizing its members, as well as those who were to carry out diversionist activities. One copy of these instructions was found on a dead German airman, a non-commissioned officer named Umbrost.[7] The contents of this document need no comment.

It must be noted that during the German-Polish war there was hardly an instance of treason among the members of any minority other than the German. This fact intensified the reaction of the Polish community and authorities against the German diversionists, especially in face of a war treacherously forced upon Poland by the Reich. But it must be added that even if, in self-defence, Poles reacted violently against the German minority's treason, there is no evidence whatever to show that any diversionists who fell into the hands of the Polish authorities were treated otherwise than in accordance with the laws of war.

---

[7] See Appendix One.

CHAPTER THREE - THE TRUTH ABOUT THE BYDGOSZCZ INCIDENTS

THE German propaganda has endeavoured to convince international opinion that on September 3, 1939, the Poles carried out a wholesale massacre of the innocent German population of Bydgoszcz (Bromberg). The German lies about the alleged Polish atrocities (*Polnische Greueltaten*) have long since been refuted. We give in this chapter a certain number of depositions and eye-witness accounts, which tell the true story of these events. They reveal that, at the beginning of the war, German diversionist agents organized a rising in Bydgoszcz, and that this attempt was partly suppressed the same day in the centre of the town. Taken together, the depositions prove that the total number of German killed in the whole district did not exceed four hundred.

The first deposition comes from an English lady, Miss Baker-Beall, who was living at Bydgoszcz at the beginning of the war:

"Friday, first September, was the first air raid on Bydgoszcz, followed by a second, when I was out in the town. Returning home when it was over I counted six large fires in the town, they seemed to be all civilian buildings. So far as I know no military damage was done. During the last few days large numbers of Germans must have entered Bydgoszcz secretly across the 'green frontier' and from Danzig.

"Evidently large quantities of arms, rifles, and machine-guns had been smuggled across the frontier and concealed in the town or its environs, for from this day on the Germans in large numbers began sniping from the windows of German houses and flats, and continued it day and night till the entry of the German forces; from the third on they also did machine-gunning from the roofs, and fired upon everything, men, women, horses (fortunately children were seldom in the streets). A dead horse lay in our street for two days because it was too dangerous to take it away. Opposite a Red Cross station which I three times visited was a German house and the inhabitants fired on it continually though the Red Cross flag was displayed, when the stretcher-bearers were bringing in casualties.

"1.9. On this day two Germans, father and son, were shot in our street as they were in possession of hand-grenades, and when challenged by soldiers ran away and fired at them.

"The soldiers shot them.

"Also I was told that the German proprietor of a chemist's shop was arrested and shot for being in possession of a hand-grenade. Another hand-grenade was exploded within a few yards of a shop where I was making purchases.

"This was only the beginning, afterwards the cases were too numerous to be noted.

"2.9. There were six or possibly seven air raids on this day. Two were driven off by Polish planes, but the others got in and apparently did little damage.

"It was, I think, on this day, that the decision was made to arm the citizens of the town, as the soldiers were being withdrawn. The order came from Warsaw to the town President, but there seems to have been some over-haste and perhaps a little confusion in carrying it out, for it was said (and I believe with truth) that many Germans represented themselves as loyal citizens and received arms, for certainly afterwards the sniping seemed to greatly increase.

"The President (Mayor of the Town), Mr. Barciszewski, also received the order to go at once to Warsaw with all municipal documents and funds, and left the town in his car just before the Germans entered it.

"The report was immediately spread by the Germans that he had absconded with all the town treasures and was responsible for the death of many German citizens.[8]

"'Blut Sonntag.' 3.9. The so-called 'Bloody Sunday,' has, of course, been the theme of much lying German propaganda concerning Bromberg-

---

[8] Hearing of this charge he returned after a time to defend his honour and was arrested by the Germans together with his wife and son, who was quite a youth. He was kept prisoner for some time and then had a pretence of a trial (by court martial, I believe). The charges mentioned were brought against him and upheld, although he produced evidence that he had strictly carried out official orders. He was condemned to death and finally shot after having been treated in a shameful and humiliating way, so that he constantly begged to have the judgment carried out immediately. The fate of his wife and son remained for some time doubtful. Just before leaving Bydgoszcz I was told that the wife had been released, but the son was still in prison. Another version was that he had been shot, but I never learned what had actually happened to him,

Bydgoszcz, and it was on this day that I was shot at for the first time, but not hurt.

"I was in the streets off and on from 9 a.m. to about 4 p.m., having gone out to see friends and to enquire how they had got through Saturday's bombing.

"There was a good deal of bombing on this day and I had to take shelter two or three times, which delayed my return. Between 1 and 2 p.m. I went to the house of an acquaintance as the bombing was beginning again, and there heard that about an hour or so before I arrived a detachment of Polish artillery drove quietly through the main street past this house, evidently in retreat and on their way to join the forces beyond the town. They were followed soon after by a battery at a smart pace which had covered their retreat and were now hastening to rejoin them. As they passed a German house on the opposite side there was a burst of firing from the windows; the officer gave the order to halt, turned a gun upon the house and fired, whereupon the sniping ceased and the battery continued on its way.

"After this the civilian guards arrested all Germans whom they found with arms in their possession and they were shot out of hand.

"While we were talking a member of the household came home from church and said that there had been sniping from the turrets of the Jesuit Church in the Old Market, as the congregation left the church, and here again arrests were made and the people with arms shot, but I saw no signs of atrocities.

"The German accounts later spoke of fierce fighting going on in the streets adjacent to the main street where this artillery affair took place, but I stood at the door of a house in one of these streets where I had taken cover from an air raid. Looking out into the sunlit street I saw at one end an old lady and gentleman taking their dog for a walk, and at the other end I saw Polish soldiers going along in single file on both sides of the street close to the houses to get protection from the bombing planes.

"From later reports we learned that the Germans had miscalculated; they had believed that the German troops would enter the town on the 3rd, and hence the augmented shooting, as they threw off all pretence of moderation, but the troops did not appear until the afternoon of the 5th.

"About 4 p.m. I went home up the main street, stopping to watch two guns firing at three planes high overhead, but apart from that the street was perfectly quiet. Later reports explained that the frontier guards and some artillery had held up the enemy on our part of the frontier, hence the delay in their progress.

"4.9. Was a day of anxious waiting, I do not even remember whether there was an air raid.

"5.9. More air raids. I was in the town and had to take shelter three times. Finally went to a friend living in the main street. About 2 p.m. the firing became much hotter and seemed to come closer, we still thought it was increased sniping. About half an hour later, as the noise increased, one of our number went down to see what was on, and returned a few minutes later saying that the Germans were in the town.

"I at once started for home and near the place where I was fired at on Sunday saw the body of a young air-raid warden who had been shot through the head —of course, non-combatant and unarmed. Went to the Red Cross first-aid station where I saw a Red Cross stretcher-bearer dying, he had been killed by a hand-grenade, of which the Volksdeutsche seemed to have an unlimited quantity. As I was going through the street a group of people called me to take cover as sniping was going on. As I entered a house there was a flash of a rifle from an opposite window, evidently the Germans in this part of the town had not yet heard of the troops.

"When I reached home I heard that a young man and a young woman living in the house (air-raid wardens) had been shot, the man through the window of his room, he died two days later, and the woman as she left the house to go to her duties; she is crippled for life.

"From this time on life was a nightmare of horrors. The Germans started the campaign of lies about the Polish atrocities on the so-called 'Bloody Sunday,' and almost the first victims of this campaign were a number of young boy scouts, from 12 to 16 years of age, who were set up in the Old Market against the wall of the Municipal Museum and shot. No reason was given.

"A devoted priest who rushed to administer the Last Sacrament was shot too. He received five wounds. A Pole said afterwards that the sight of *those children lying dead was the most piteous of all horrors he saw. That week those murders continued. Thirty-four of the leading tradespeople and merchants of the town were shot and many other leading citizens. The square was encircled by military with machine-guns.*

"Among the thirty-four was a man whom I knew who was too ill to take any part in politics or public affairs. When the execution took place he was too weak to stand and fell down, they beat him and dragged him again to his feet.

"Another of the first victims was the seventeen-year-old only son of a well-known surgeon who had died a year before. The father had been greatly esteemed by all and had treated Poles and Germans with the same care and devotion.

"We never heard what the poor lad was accused of.

"An instance of one horrible execution was related by a friend of mine. This person was standing at a window which overlooked a garden of the Polish Club, when the tramp of feet was heard and a party of civilians entered accompanied by Gestapo and S.S.

"An order was given and the civilians formed up into a line, the observer thought they had come to go through military exercises. A second order was given and the men dropped on their knees and at a third order began to crawl to and fro on the hands and knees. Then the police began to shoot and continued shooting until the last of their prisoners lay still. The shooting was, of course, heard and there was commotion in the streets, those in the street trying to force the iron gates, and those within threatening to shoot them unless they went away. At last the commotion ceased and the people were driven away, but soon after the Gestapo were given another house outside the town.

"The shooting still goes on, but it is farther away and everyone knows what is happening.

"These are only a few examples of the indiscriminate murders which took place. The shooting was still going on when I left the town. At the beginning it was by the military, afterwards the Secret Police (Gestapo and S.S.) took it over and exceeded it in cruelty.

"When the soldiers first entered the town their minds were inflamed against the Poles by the stories of horrible atrocities which the Poles had

committed on the Germans, and in revenge they themselves acted with the most appalling savagery.

"Stories were spread of how hundreds of mutilated German corpses had been found in the forest, with eyes put out and tongues torn out of the victims, and photographs were shown to foreign newspaper correspondents of the victims of these murders.

"It was quite true that hundreds of such corpses were found, but they were of Poles, great numbers being of women and children who had fled from Bydgoszcz when the Germans approached and were hunted and machine-gunned by German airmen who had followed them. An acquaintance of mine who fled with her husband and two children, but had to return as they found no place of refuge, said that the saddest sight was the number of little corpses that strewed the way —babies and little ones who succumbed to exposure and want of food, or were shot down in the flight.

"There were corpses of Germans who had also fled, but the number was small and they would, like the Poles, be targets for the planes. It was also observed that the names of these people were printed at intervals six or eight times in the lists of victims, but were each time reckoned as fresh victims in order to lengthen the list.

"The following occurrence, told to a friend of mine by the only survivor, may illustrate this point. An old German woman and twelve other Germans decided to flee together to Brzóza, a forest place some kilometres from Bydgoszcz, and take refuge with the Catholic priest there. They were on foot, and when evening came on they were still about an hour's walk from Brzóza; they turned into a cottage in the hamlet they were passing through and decided to spend the night there. The old woman was uneasy and wished to press on, but others refused. When the others were sleeping, she got up and crept out of the house (she was a very devout Catholic and said a voice told her not to delay). When only a short distance from the house, she heard planes approaching and, turning to see where they were going, saw the cottage struck by a bomb and totally destroyed. She said that everyone in the house was killed and the corpses were terribly mutilated, but—as we see, by German planes, not by Polish murderers."

The next account is no less convincing:[9]

"On 1st and 3rd September, agents of the Gestapo, disguised as Polish peasants, police-agents, frontier-guards, etc., mingled with the evacuees, who were arriving in great numbers from the districts lying near the German frontier. In the vehicles, which were ostensibly serving for the transport of their baggage, were hidden arms, especially small machine-guns of the type employed by the German Army, and ammunition. These agents at first kept themselves concealed in houses belonging to members of a secret German association. Other agents landed by parachute at nightfall in the neighbouring forests, and it has since been ascertained that they had received orders to provoke riots at Bydgoszcz on Sunday, 3rd September, at 10 a.m. Motorized German divisions were to hold themselves in readiness outside the town, in order to occupy it in the course of the day.

"Actually, at the arranged hour, the agents of the Gestapo, aided by the German minority population of the town, attacked Polish troops who happened to be at Bydgoszcz as well as civilian Polish population which was coming out of the churches, not sparing the women and children. Shots were fired from windows and roofs of houses belonging to Germans, and even from roofs and towers of several churches. The disturbance caused by this unexpected attack did not last long. The Polish troops and the civilian population took up the pursuit of the instigators of the riot. The latter put up an embittered resistance and more than once siege had to be laid to houses where Gestapo agents had taken refuge. A veritable battle developed between the armed Germans and the Polish troops and civilians. The Germans accused of having taken part in the riots, but who had not been taken whilst in possession of arms, were brought before a court martial which sat during the entire day of 3rd September. Order was not re-established until six in the afternoon.

"According to the figures which I am in a position to refer to, the Germans left approximately 150 dead on the field, of which only a part were citizens of Bydgoszcz. The rest was composed of unknown men, doubtless agents, who had come from the Reich. About forty people were

---

[9] Deposition No. 512.

brought before the court martial, which condemned fourteen of them to death. There were also numerous victims among the Polish Population.

"After having crushed the putsch, the Polish troops remained at Bydgoszcz during the whole of the following night and the morning of Monday, 4th September, but as their retreat had been decided by the authorities in command, they left the town during the day, and it was definitely occupied by Germans from 5th September.

"Immediately after their entry, the massacres of the Polish population commenced. Without trial, and often in a revolting manner, the Germans shot a great number of the most prominent citizens of the town, among them several women and priests, as well as the members of the civic guard organized by the population after the retreat of the Polish troops. The number of victims augmented from day to day, and in the course of a few weeks it surpassed, in Bydgoszcz alone, the figure of three thousand.

"One of the cruellest episodes of those days was the execution of a group of Polish boy scouts who had been arrested by agents of the Gestapo, either because they were in the uniform of the boy scouts, or because their uniforms had been discovered during house-to-house searches. These poor children, unaware of the doom that awaited them, joked and even played games among themselves after their arrest. They realized the truth when they were made to line up on the Market Square and the machine-guns were brought. Some of the little ones began to cry, but the others gave proof of the most admirable courage. They intoned the Polish national anthem, 'Jeszcze Polska nie zginela' and fell like heroes, machine-gunned at close quarters by the Germans."

Witness No. 3 was employed at Bydgoszcz, and was at work throughout this period.[i] He declares:

"On that memorable Sunday which the Germans have christened 'the bloody Sunday of Bydgoszcz,' the German regular army had not yet arrived in the town.

"At ten in the morning the German population suddenly opened fire on the detachment of Polish National Guards which was in the town and on any Polish civilians who happened to be passing through the streets. The fire was so sustained, so violent and unexpected that it at once caused a panic. All who could do so took shelter in houses. The firing came from private houses occupied by Germans, and also from the tower of the Protestant church, where, as we later observed, a cleverly concealed machine-gun had been placed. As the firing did not cease for a single moment, we had to proceed to the attack. We first disposed of the nest in the church, damaging the tower somewhat in doing so. Simultaneously an attack was made on the men hidden in the German houses. There were losses on both sides. We had to force our way into the locked and bolted houses where men dressed in civilian clothes received us with heavy fire. These people, who so far had lived in perfect amity with us, now, after twenty years of living on the same soil, showed us their real features.

"How did it come to pass that the civilian population began to fight our soldiers, when they were bound to realize that in face of the crushing numerical superiority of the Polish elements in Bydgoszcz the attempt was doomed to failure? That will always remain a mystery to us. Either the Germans had overestimated their strength, or else they were badly informed as to the proximity of the German troops. It may be that the Germans in Bydgoszcz wished to free 'the town by their own efforts in order to welcome the German troops to a free' Bydgoszcz and to earn special praise.

"The total killed was not large. No harm was done to civilians who had not committed any crime. Accounts were settled only with those who were taken with arms. There were altogether 160 Germans. By far the majority of these fell in combat, the others were shot after a summary court martial.

"Among those killed were only a few inhabitants of Bydgoszcz. The rest were strangers, probably part of the Hitler troops who, acting under orders from their command, had succeeded in filtering into the town together with the Polish refugees who during those days had arrived in large numbers. The local German population provided them with arms and assigned them their posts. Everything proves that the affair had been prepared a long time before by the 'competent' elements.

"The firing began at ten in the morning, but it did not cease till six in the evening. By this time the centre of the town was in our hands. Absolute calm reigned in that part of Bydgoszcz where I was.

"At 7.30 that same evening the Polish commander of the Pomorze front telephoned an order to the civil authorities to evacuate the town immediately. I left Bydgoszcz at nine o'clock; on the road outside the town I was fired on by German machine-guns.

"From September 3rd to 7th inclusive I was in the immediate neighbourhood of Bydgoszcz; I was continually in contact with inhabitants of the town, and no information whatever came to my knowledge of acts of cruelty or of outrages upon dead bodies. Beyond the 160 killed whom I have mentioned, there were no other victims. The German Army first entered Bydgoszcz only on September 4th, at 12.30, but, for some unknown reason, they retired almost immediately. They returned next day, Tuesday, September 5. All the representatives of the intelligentsia class were at once arrested, including the clergy. Priest X. Y., known to everybody and held in great esteem in the town, was chased barefoot along the street; he was ordered to march at the point of bayonets and to call upon the population through a megaphone not to resist the German authorities. The missionary fathers received still worse treatment. Their new, uncompleted church was turned into stables, and two of their priests were killed.

"M. Fiedler, President of the National Party, the solicitor Typrowicz, and a great number of members of the Association of Insurgents and Combatants were also killed, as well as several active members of the Association of the West. Among others, for instance, the well-known family of the publisher and editor, M. Teska, were deported with the clergy into the heart of Germany.

"It is not known who instigated the movement to assemble the Polish boy scouts in the Square. When quite a number had been collected a machine-gun was set up to fire on them. The lads were not intimidated, and showed courage in the face of death; as they fell they cried 'Long live Poland!'

"The Dean of Bydgoszcz, Father Stepczynski, an old man almost in his seventies, was also murdered.

"It was not until after September 10th that there was a certain slackening in the tension.

"A new period of terror set in on October l0th. The last representatives of the intelligentsia were arrested, also several solicitors, doctors, and women known for their social activities.

"Many of these persons were murdered during the first fortnight of November.

"On November 11th, the National Holiday in celebration of Poland's liberation, the Mayor of Bydgoszcz, M. Barciszewski, was shot. It is particularly worthy of note that he had not been at Bydgoszcz during the German rising, and returned to the town only after the German military campaign in Poland was closed."

Here is another account:[10]

"Having heard in Bydgoszcz of the formation of volunteer detachments, I presented myself at No. 14 Jarnicki Street, and was accepted. We were supplied with weapons at the County Offices. Thence we were sent to the Police headquarters at Jagiellonska Street. As we were going in we were fired on by machine-guns from the roofs of houses opposite. We were formed into small detachments which, with several soldiers, were sent to various parts of the town where German civilians were firing on Poles. On arrival we proceeded to make a search, and German civilians taken with arms in hand were shot on the spot."

A fifth deposition:[11]

"At Bydgoszcz the mutual relations between the German minority and the Poles were good. The situation began to change only about a fortnight before the war, as the rumour was spreading that in the event of war the local German population was preparing some step. In fact, the Bydgoszcz Germans began, as though by command, to spread the rumour that Poland would lose the war with Germany and that there was no other chance of salvation except to hand Danzig, part of Pomorze, and other Western provinces over to Germany. The Poles began to notice that the Germans were meeting more and more frequently among themselves, and that there were increasing numbers of German departures either for Germany, or for Danzig.

---

[10] First-Class Soldier of Tank Division, R. J., Deposition No. 485.
[11] Engineer K. P., Deposition No. 30.

"The incidents which occurred in Bydgoszcz during the early days of the war fully confirmed the Polish suspicions and fears. It was seen that German families who had protested their loyalty to Poland also took part in the conspiracy against the State. For instance, there were Germans originally settled at Łódź, who had made their home in Bydgoszcz, such as the Neumanns, the Hamans, and the Matzes. On the eve of the war one of the Hamans, a reservist who had been called up to the Polish Army, fled to Danzig. When the German troops entered Bydgoszcz Oswald Haman turned up in S.A. uniform. Shots were fired at Polish detachments from the Hamans' and Matzes' houses. Many of the people working in the Pfefferkorn furniture factory took part in the anti-Polish conspiracy. There was also firing at Poles from the Pfefferkorn house.

"September 1st passed quietly on the whole. Except for brief German air-raids on the Bydgoszcz aerodrome there was no incident worth mentioning. But the town was filled with rumours that the Germans were preparing a rising.

"On September 2nd, between 11 and 12 in the morning, there was an air raid which demolished part of the barracks of the 61st Regiment. During the afternoon the rumour spread that the Germans would be entering the town at any moment, and that the rising would begin immediately. There were hardly any Germans to be seen in the streets. During the afternoon groups of Germans, each numbering from 30 to 150 persons, who were to have started diversionist operations, began to arrive from the frontier, convoyed by police reservists. They were all brought from the direction of Inowroclaw. The people greeted them with hostile and menacing shouts, but the police allowed no excesses whatever. During the night of September 2nd / 3rd Germans making light signals were arrested in Bydgoszcz. The people had no sleep that night, being excited by rumours that the enemy was approaching and by the acts committed by German diversionists.

"The first shots were fired in Bydgoszcz on September 3rd between 4 and 5 in the morning. At 5 I learned that diversionist operations had begun. As commander of the local civilian defence, I sent men to the streets in the centre of the town. There could be no question of our gaining control of the outskirts. In Danzig Street and on Liberty Square two of my men *were wounded. Shots were fired at the Poles from inside houses. It was now past six o'clock. Until seven o'clock there was comparative calm, broken only by single shots from time to time. The population was in a state of panic, believing that the German rising, accompanied by diversionist acts, had already begun. In Jagiellonska Street one of the most prominent representatives of these German elements, the retired director of the municipal abattoirs, was killed.*

"A little detachment of Poles commanded by a Second Lieutenant entered the town at seven o'clock. Along the entire length of Danzig Street and from the side streets (from St. John's Street as far as the department store) a heavy fire was directed against the detachment. Fortunately none of them was wounded. Then I saw a group of Germans, some forty of them, armed with rifles and revolvers, running. Among them I noticed three Bydgoszcz Germans whom I knew by sight. They ran along Sniadecki Street from the direction of Piastowski Square. Without doubt they were intending to attack the Lieutenant's detachment, as well as my men. They fired as they ran. Several Germans fell. The Second Lieutenant was also wounded. We captured twenty-two Germans and conducted them to the barracks of the 61st Regiment.

"At eight o'clock I saw the representative of the chief of police. He gave me a letter from the administrative head of the county, Suski. Around the county office and indeed everywhere in the town there was confusion. Firing was going on on all sides, from Poles as well as from Germans. A German disguised as a Polish captain contributed to the panic in front of the county offices. He ran along the street, shouting: 'The Germans are coming.' He was killed, and on him was found an armlet with a swastika and a German First-Lieutenant's document. The firing grew heavier. It was clear beyond doubt that numerous groups of organized assailants were taking part in the action throughout the town. At that moment I heard that they had killed engineer Grodzki.

"From the county offices I went through Gymnasium Street and Liberty Square towards the headquarters of the State police. Bullets were flying from all directions. It was 9.30. I did not find anyone at the police headquarters. The building was under continuous fire from the Protestant church on Koscielecki Square. The Germans had got a machine-gun in this

church. The headquarters telephone was ringing incessantly. I arranged for calls to be answered. It transpired that Poles were ringing from all parts of the town, reporting the houses from which firing was coming. I got forty sheets of addresses taken down, and thus we were able to organize a counter-attack. I destroyed these lists only when the Germans entered Warsaw. I recall inter alia that we were informed of firing directed against the station from a disused brewery opposite, in Station Street, and that one report stated that men were organizing diversionist activities in the Protestant cemetery, in the German sailing club which was close to the gasworks, etc.

"We continually sent small mixed detachments of soldiers and police to the spots from which we had reports. One of these detachments brought back a machine-gun which they had captured from the Germans on Koscielecki Square. Germans encountered bearing arms were shot on the spot; suspects were sent mainly to the barracks of the 61st Regiment. With a detachment of ten to twelve men I myself tackled the Protestant cemetery. As we entered it a shot was fired. But we found nobody there. Only in the cemetery keeper's house, where we found a revolver and cartridges, did we discover a German who could not establish his identity. This cemetery was searched a second time by detachments of National Defence Guards. I next went with my detachment to the gasworks. The German club was in ruins. It appears that a large number of German attackers fell at this spot. A strict search had been made of all the houses going from Tornow towards the station, and all the occupants of every house had to show their documents. I recall that in the third house from Tornow we found six Germans from neighbouring villages in hiding. Everywhere, in the course of these searches, other detachments arrested Germans who had come from Nakło, Świecie, and other localities in the vicinity of Bydgoszcz. They had been ordered to present themselves on September 3rd. Without doubt that was the date fixed for the beginning of the German diversionist activities.

"Early in the afternoon we mastered the situation in the centre of the town. Three detachments had shared among them the task of quelling the revolt: (1) the groups of the National Guards; (2) my detachment; (3) that of Second Lieutenant S. Altogether we had a thousand men at the most. But

the situation was very different on the outskirts of the town, and in the neighbouring villages which our patrols did not reach and where generally speaking the Germans remained in command all the time.

"While this action was in progress I continually saw groups of German aggressors, consisting of eight, ten or fifteen men escorted by our men. Between 2.30 and 6.30 in the afternoon the chief of police took 92,000 złotys from the Germans, which sum he afterwards sent to the general command of the police at Włocławek. So large a sum sufficiently proved that those who had come from outside Bydgoszcz had been generously paid for their 'patriotic' labour.

"During the many searches which I made I was struck by one characteristic detail: we succeeded in getting hold of the culprits only in certain of the houses from which firing had come. It was only later, when I was at Warsaw, that I realized why. In almost every one of these houses hiding-places had been constructed in advance, and these were excellently camouflaged, so that they could not be seen from outside. Thus, in the Pfefferkorn house, from which firing came continually, there was a hiding-place on the second floor.

"During the retreat on September 5th I saw thirty groups of these Germans at Włocławek (each group numbered between 150 and 200 men). They were to be placed in a concentration camp. I learned later that the German troops had recaptured them all from us."

Another deposition:[12]

"On September 3rd I rose as usual in the morning to go to the factory where I had been in charge for the past six months. In the street I saw mobilization posters and realized that I was called up. So I went back home to put on my uniform. The day was hot and I had the window open. At 9.30 I heard an aeroplane, and immediately afterwards a ragged fusillade of shots. I got into my car and drove to the factory. As I went I distinguished rapid firing which sounded like a machine-gun above the fusillade. In the street I came across small disorderly groups of soldiers moving and lines of vehicles which seemed to be in a panic, and a captain who was trying to stop them. I gave up the idea of going to the factory and,

---

[12] J. P., Lieutenant, Deposition No. 31.

turning to good account the fact that I was already in uniform, I reassembled the fleeing soldiers and went with them to the town command. There I found two officers attempting to make contact with the administrative authorities and the police.

"Meantime information was coming in which enabled us more or less to understand what was happening. It was clear that the Germans were carrying out diversionist activities. We set to work to organize patrols which we sent in various directions in accordance with the news which came in.

"We made contact with an infantry company of one of the Bydgoszcz regiments, the 61st or 69th, which reached the town command at 11.30. With its aid we gradually began to master the situation, making searches in those houses from which firing was reported, or which had given shelter to the aggressors. We arrested German suspects, who were afterwards escorted to the town command. At one o'clock there were 150 of these. The search resulted in the discovery of a hand-grenade, two military maps, and several cuttings from German papers published in the Reich. I took part in five house searches, but without result.

"As I drove around the town in my car I came to the conclusion that the diversionist operations attempted by the Germans were intended inter alia to spread confusion and panic in the rear of the Polish troops. They fired from the attic windows and lofts, that is, when they were able to do so in safety, and well concealed, but firing must have been difficult in view of the spots where they were probably hidden. It is also certain that a large number of Germans had taken part in the affair. There can be no suggestion that there was any question whatever of provocation on the part of the Polish authorities or army. The civil authorities had left Bydgoszcz before the affair began. The attempt was spontaneously crushed by us, that is, by the two commanders of the town command, myself and several officers of the infantry company. I saw only two Polish dead lying in front of the church, on the other hand, I saw not one German killed or wounded. Some of the Germans escorted to the town command had light grazes, a fact which I must underline. They were not even worth dressing.

"The captured Germans were to have been transported out of the town and into the interior of the country. But I don't know whether this was done, for, before three in the afternoon I left via Inowroclaw in the direction of Warsaw, where my regiment was stationed. On the way, outside Bydgoszcz, I met a detachment of police hastening towards the town. Much later, at Wilno, I met the engineer Z., who told me he had remained in Bydgoszcz until the early hours of September 4th. According to his story absolute calm prevailed until the night. At two o'clock, just before dawn, he heard shots. At daybreak he learned that a large band of German agents on bicycles had attempted to get to the centre of the town from the direction of the station, but they had been repulsed by the army and had left their bicycles and materials behind."

Here is a priest's deposition:[13]

"The Germans talk a great deal about 'Bloody Sunday' at Bydgoszcz, and pretend that there were some 2000 German victims of the massacre. But they ignore the fact that they had themselves provoked the Poles to execute 150 Germans who fired from ambush upon Polish troops.

"On Sunday, September 3rd, at ten in the morning the Germans opened fire from the tops of the towers of the Protestant churches, from hiding-places, and from the roofs of their houses at retreating Polish troops. Not at all numerous at Bydgoszcz, they none the less ventured upon this rising because they believed the Polish Army was being closely followed by the German Army, which was already at Nakło (some thirty kilometres from Bydgoszcz) on Friday, September 1st. Now, the German troops did not penetrate into Bydgoszcz until September 5th. The obvious provocation committed by the Bydgoszcz Germans could not go unpunished. The angry population denounced these Germans to the Polish soldiers. It is only just that they were shot. The Protestant church at Szwederowo (a suburb of Bydgoszcz) was burned down, a machine-gun having been fired from its tower. The pastor at Czyzkówek suburb, who allowed a machine-gun to be mounted on his church, was shot. Close on 150 rebels altogether perished at this time. (This figure was given by the men who took the bodies to the cemetery.)

---

[13] Father X.Y., Deposition No. 40.

"The Germans' vengeance after they had taken Bydgoszcz knew no bounds. It would be difficult to say how many Poles were shot. But it was over 5000."

A cavalry officer states:[14]

"On September 3rd about ten in the morning I had to conduct General Skotnicki to the command of the 15th Infantry Division at Bydgoszcz. We drove in two cars to Bydgoszcz, from our quarters at Myślęcinek. But we could not drive along the main street, namely, Danzig Street, for we were greeted with numerous single bursts of machine-gun fire. One machine-gun was mounted on the tower of the Protestant church, on Liberty Square. Thence it dominated the centre of the town. It is necessary to state that that day our front line was at least fifty kilometres from Bydgoszcz, and that there was no garrison whatever at this town, beyond a small battalion of our National Guards.

"Being unable to enter Bydgoszcz by Danzig Street, our cars made their way round the town close to Bielawka in order to enter by the road from Fordon. While we were making this detour we were greeted with isolated shots coming from a large German factory, of which I have forgotten the name.

"I know from my non-commissioned officer, W., who had reached the centre of the town, having left before us to find petrol, that accounts were settled solely with Germans who had been taken in the act of firing or who had had weapons. I declare that returning in the afternoon of the same day, September 3rd, from the Divisional Command, situated at Foch Street, to our quarters, I went right along Danzig Street. This was after the suppression of the German rising, and I noticed only a few bodies in civilian clothes before the 'Under the Eagle' hotel.

"As Danzig Street was the centre of the disturbances, stories which tell of the numerous executions of which the German population have been victims are pure invention, for I was on the spot immediately after these incidents, and the traces of what had occurred could not have been removed so quickly."

---

[14] Lieutenant J. S. of the cavalry brigade, Deposition No. 14.

A baker, F. A., a foreign citizen, testifies:[15]

"Anyone who witnessed the events which occurred in Poland after the outbreak of hostilities and afterwards followed the story of these events only in the German Press is able to realize all the extent of the misfortune which Poland has so cruelly suffered.

"The German invasion not only caused the deaths of Poland's best sons, the physical torture of those who remained alive and the destruction of material goods. The Germans have not hesitated before the foulest of defamation to represent the Poles as such a barbarous nation that they have behaved with the utmost cruelty towards the unarmed German population. And Poland could only be silent in reply.

"It is not long since I returned to my country (Jugoslavia), where I have been able to testify as an eye-witness to the incidents which occurred at Bydgoszcz on September 3rd, 1939, the day called 'Bloody Sunday.' In the Press here and also the European Press I have found only information on the subject of 'Bloody Sunday' which in no way corresponded to the truth. That is why I have decided to tell what I saw or what was seen by witnesses whom I know to be trustworthy.

"In the night of Saturday to Sunday (2nd to 3rd September) the Polish troops fell back along Danzig Street, the main street of the town. The troops were followed by civil population fleeing from neighbouring villages. According to these people the German troops were some three kilometres to the north and west of the town. On Sunday morning all the main streets were crowded with people fleeing in the direction of Inowroclaw and Lekno, but only a very few troops were left.

"The Polish civil population did not possess any arms. Suddenly about eleven o'clock in the morning innumerable rifle shots were fired at the civil population and the rest of the troops, from house roofs, from the towers of the Protestant church, those of the Jesuits' church, from the old market, and the Protestant cemetery.

"Machine-guns were mounted on the tower of the Protestant church, on Liberty Square, on the roof of the large shop at the corner of Dworcowa Street and Danzig Street, and on the tower of the Jesuits' church and that of the Protestant church on Koscielecki Square. Bydgoszcz Germans as

---

[15] F. A. (a foreigner), Deposition No. 51.

well as others from neighbouring villages, all of them equipped with arms, were in ambush on the roofs of private houses. As Germans captured on Sunday afternoon and Monday avowed, the Germans were to enter Bydgoszcz on Sunday afternoon. So they had begun to fire to provoke a panic, to disorganize the Polish troops and to spread terror among the civil population. But during Saturday night Polish troops advanced towards Bydgoszcz from the south-east. Swinging round to the south of Bydgoszcz, the Polish troops succeeded in attacking the German troops in the west of the town on their flank. They managed to drive the Germans back westward and to the south of Koronowo some forty kilometres to the south-west of Bydgoszcz. The Germans failed to enter Bydgoszcz on the Sunday, and it was the Polish Army which returned. But the Bydgoszcz Germans did not stop shooting. They were invested by the Polish troops, who cleared the houses and roofs of the armed Germans.

"The Germans who did not perish on the spot were tried by courts martial and shot. And that was the 'bloody Sunday' of Bydgoszcz, September 3rd, 1939. It was not the Poles who organized a pogrom of the Germans, for the Polish civil population did not possess weapons. On the contrary, it was the German minority which, taking up arms and occupying positions dominating the town, fired on the Polish troops.

"So it is quite understandable that when the Polish soldiers returned more than one German perished.

"The fact that the Poles committed no atrocity against the Germans captured with weapons in their hands has been testified to by a German doctor. He reported that he had examined the bodies and had found no trace of ill-treatment."

CHAPTER FOUR - PARACHUTISTS AND DIVERSIONISTS ATTACHED TO THE GERMAN ARMED FORCES

General Observations

THE German diversionist activities in all their multifarious forms and considerable dimensions constitute a unique feature in the history of war. They played a primary role in the success of the German Army's offensive, and were meticulously prepared long before the war.

Parachute descents were only one of the methods by means of which diversionist agents were deposited behind the Polish lines. In any case, there is nothing to indicate that the number dropped in this way exceeded fifteen persons at any given point.

The activities carried out by the agents as part of the German Army's methods of fighting consisted of:

1. The utilization everywhere of the German minority, which was thoroughly acquainted with the given region and terrain.
2. The descent of parachutists in small groups at a large number of spots situated in the front line, as well as behind the lines often at a great distance from the actual fighting.

It must be especially emphasized that the Germans' subversive activities were particularly favoured by the fact that the Polish authorities were too slow in arresting elements suspected of conduct injurious to the State. It is now known that this attitude arose from a fear that Germany might exploit any such preventive measures as a proof of Poland's bellicose intentions. It is very probable that Germany's charges of alleged persecution of the German minority in Poland were provoked by the fear that the Polish authorities might discover that minority's subversive activity, prepared with such detailed care by the German aggressors.

The diversionist activities reached such great proportions primarily because when hostilities broke out the Polish mobilization was not completed, and in consequence the various defence units, civil and military, were still in a state of reorganization. The higher commands did not have sufficiently organized supporting troops at their disposal in the rear, as their mobilization had been planned to take place during the days following. Finally, the general mobilization itself was hindered by the work of the enemy air force, which started to bomb all over the country, even as Hitler was making solemn promises to abstain from such bombings. And this facilitated the Germans' diversionist activities.

Pre-War Organization of Subversive Activities

A document which fell into Polish hands the day after hostilities began, i.e. on September 2,[16] provided definite proof that these activities were very carefully planned before the war, and of the leading role assigned to the German minority. Members of the minority serving in the Polish Army as well as civilian elements were utilized.

Examination of the diversionist agents taken prisoner provided the following details of the organization of their activities:

1. The agents were recruited mainly from the youth group known as the *Hitler Jugend* and from men and women, chiefly of German nationality, enrolled from Poland.
2. Special courses lasting from two weeks to three months were organized for these agents on the territory of the Reich.
3. Those who took these courses were divided into two categories. The first, consisting of persons with a thorough knowledge of the Polish language, was charged with special missions to be carried out in the rear of the Polish Army. The second category consisted of persons who were to mingle with the crowds of Polish civilian refugees fleeing from the war and the bombing attacks.
4. A short time before the war the students at these courses underwent a supplementary training in special camps, where they were assigned to "districts of diversionist activity."

---

[16] See Appendix One.

Besides the agents recruited from the youth and intended to collaborate with the German civilian population, there was a group of directors and instructors composed of officers who arrived in Poland, provided with passports, a little before the war, and of local agents transported by car or aeroplane to the rear of the Polish armies during the first days of the war.

Depositions and Statements

One of the German diversionist agents, a lad aged 18, captured near Włódżimierz in Wolhynia, Eastern Poland, made the following statement:[17]

"In December, 1938, members of the Hitler Jugend were summoned to attend a three months' course. They received training in the use of parachutes, as well as in liaison work with the Reich air force. The students were told that in the event of war they would be assigned to espionage activities. For this purpose they would be transported into the enemy country, where they would have to identify the positions of the enemy armies, etc., and to supply the German airmen with details by means of agreed signals.

"This activity was obligatory upon the members of the Hitler-Jugend who participated in the course; at the time of mobilization they were to receive notices similar to those of ordinary mobilization.

"The subversive agents were divided into two categories. The first was composed of persons possessing a thorough knowledge of Polish. They were supplied with Polish officers' and non-commissioned officers' uniforms, or those of Polish police or railroad officials. In these uniforms they were dropped by parachutes on Polish territory. The second category was composed of those who knew Polish only imperfectly. They were dropped in civilian clothes, and were allotted the task of mingling with the Polish refugees who streamed towards the centre of the country.

"Towards the middle of August, about fifteen days before the opening of hostilities, the students were assembled and sent to special camps, where they remained until the war started. Here they had a

---

[17] Statement No. 315.

refresher course in the plans of activity, and were assigned to various localities of Poland. (Desantenbezirke.)"

The agent in question knew only the Kaszuban dialect, and had been classed in the second category and was to pass as a "refugee from Gdynia."

He was dropped from an aeroplane in the district of Toruń, and had orders to mingle with the refugees and to proceed to the region of Zamość, Hrubieszów, and still farther east to Włódźimierz in Wolhynia. A number of German agents were directed to this region, unknown to one another.

Each agent received a list of Germans living in Poland, to whom he was to turn for aid and assistance. The author of this statement went to one named Zielke, a member of the German minority in Hrubieszów. He succeeded in fulfilling his task, furnishing the German airmen with information as to the positions of the Polish commands, their depots, stores, etc.

Agreed signals were made in the following ways:

- In the daytime, by means of tent canvas or by setting fire to stacks of hay or straw.
- At night, by means of electric torches and by setting fire to various objects.

N.B.—This statement gives no details of the way in which information obtained by agents was transmitted to the German airmen. But from other depositions it is clear that the information was transmitted by wireless as well as by light signals, which the German minority had every facility for making.

The following deposition was made by a Polish Major:[18]

"German diversionist activity in Poznań, and especially in Pomorze, was organized and prepared long before the outbreak of the war, which fact confirms that the Germans systematically prepared for the war on Poland.

---

[18] Major J. Z., Deposition No. 4.

"The main element used in German subversive activities was the youth, who were devoted to National Socialism. The young generation of Germans had perfect freedom to organize and to receive instruction in the German schools, and were almost entirely under the influence of the competent elements from the Reich. The technique of instruction to groups intended for diversionist activities was as follows: the candidate clandestinely left Poland in order to receive the necessary training in Germany. The first stage of the journey made by the future agents was Danzig. Here the German Consul-General took over their documents for safe custody, registered them, and sent them on to special points where the diversionist courses were being held. These centres were situated in Danzig, Piła (Schneidemühl), Koenigsberg, and Stettin.

"The German preparation of these agents reached wholesale proportions as soon as the Reich had solved the Czech problem. Plans for subversive action in Poland were not limited to training the cadres, but were extended to other fields of operation. Always, however, they were based on the German element, which often, irrespective of the social class to which it belonged, was engaged in employment which favoured Germany's plans. After the Czech conflict one characteristic detail could be observed. The large German landed estates definitely stopped selling their grain, especially oats and hay, though there was no economic motive for holding up sales. They were preparing provisioning bases for when the German troops should march into Poland. At a time when German propaganda was harping on the theme of 'the persecutions of the German minority in Poland' there were instances of German landed proprietors burning agricultural plant, as happened in Szubin and Wyrzysk, in order to furnish arguments for this propaganda.

"Those destined to carry out diversionist activities were even equipped to some extent, and wore brassards of an agreed colour with a yellow circle on a red or blue ground on their arms under their coats, or on their shirts. Their activity everywhere conformed to the same military instructions, to the same regulations, and everywhere they used agreed passwords.

"They terrorized even the peaceable elements of the German population, and in any case provoked disturbances and committed terroristic acts.

"On September 2nd I examined some twenty of these diversionist agents taken in the act. There could be no doubt about them, as they all wore the brassards already mentioned on their arms under their raincoats. They admitted that they had crossed the frontier during the night, close to Nakło, and that they had been charged with impeding the evacuation of the Polish Army, carrying out diversionist work and destroying means of communication. They had all been through the appropriate course in Germany. And the fact that it was possible to capture a relatively large number of them in so short a time indicates their numerical importance. Many of them penetrated into the Poznań and Pomorze areas.

"According to my information the Germans responsible for the action in Bydgoszcz on September 3rd were directed by Dr. Gersdorff, who played an important part in the organization of the Deutsche Vereinigung. It is also very clear that all the family of the owners of Café Grey and also of one Dietman participated actively. The revolt was crushed, but in consequence of its repression, which was in the nature of a spontaneous reaction, there were bound to be victims. I am sure, none the less, that the number was not large."

The following depositions add in various ways to the foregoing information:

From an aide-de-camp to a Polish Army commander:[19]
"So far as diversionist activities in south-eastern Poland were concerned, they were prepared in advance, and only carried to completion by agents dropped by parachutes. German espionage was organized by special emissaries who, disguised as Wanderlehrer (itinerant teachers), trained spies and diversionist agents. Every year several young Germans left each German colony to go to the Reich. There they received special instruction and, on their return to Poland, made the amende honorable. They went to the starosta, the administrative head of the county, and

---

[19] Lieutenant S. W., aide-de-camp to a commander in the Polish 7th Army Corps, Deposition No. 407.

talked of the cruelties of the Nazis, and expressed their joy at returning to their 'dear country.' But these same Germans remained in constant touch with and supplied information to their agents in Germany, either by post or through the Wanderlehrer. The espionage network was excellently organized and there were several such specially trained agents in every German colony.

"On September 9th a baker named Daum was arrested at Stryj and was found to have a secret wireless transmitter in his house. The deputy mayor of the German colony at Kalsdorff, or Kazalin, in Stryj district, situated on the frontier between Poland and Hungary, enjoyed general esteem and had been awarded the Cross for Merit. He was captured by the frontier-guard in the very act of handing a detailed plan of Polish troop dispositions at Tuchola, Klimace, and Ławoczne, as well as plans of projected demolitions, to an emissary of the enemy. This German and the emissary were shot on September 10th."

From a Polish Lieutenant:[20]

"There was a section of assault Storm Troops for the town and district of Bielsko. It was in action on September 1st. Information concerning the detachment had been collected ever since July, 1939. It was recruited among the German civilian population of the area.

"They fought courageously and desperately. They fired mainly from houses and various fortified positions. They were armed with carbines, revolvers, and automatics. Generally speaking their fire was not very effective. They had been trained as reserve officers and non-commissioned officers in the Polish Army, and some had been trained in Germany. They were of great diversity of age, and had a mixed collection of weapons: revolvers of various types, hand machine-guns, and hand-grenades. In all the villages inhabited by German colonists there were skirmishes between the Germans and Polish troops making a fighting retreat."

---

[20] Lieutenant D. M., Infantry Regiment, Deposition No. 281.

From a Polish Magistrate:[21]

"As an examining magistrate at Cracow I dealt with espionage cases, and I was able to determine that as the war drew closer their number increased. The Germans recruited a large number of agents from among elements of German origin inhabiting Upper Silesia and working in German Silesia."

From an officer of the Polish Army General Staff:[22]

"From intercepted documents as well as the depositions of airmen brought down and diversionist agents arrested, it is clear that the Germans made men and women whom they had brought from Poland take part in courses for parachutists, saboteurs, and agents to report on troop movements."

From a Polish Second Lieutenant:[23]

"The task of the German armies was greatly facilitated by the subversive activity of German agents who were dropped on Polish territory before the outbreak of war and during its course. For instance, the descent carried out at night in the Miechów district. These agents were recruited mainly from Germans living in Silesia who had deserted from the Polish Army. One of the minority agents killed at Tarnówskie Gory had served in the 11th Polish Infantry Regiment and had deserted to Germany a week before the war."

From a Polish Lieutenant Colonel on the Staff of an Army Corps:[24]

"Some days before the war, a vast organization of German espionage was discovered in the district of Łódź. Among other things found were explosives concealed in tins of food."

From a Polish Lieutenant:[25]

"On August 28th, 1939, that is, four days before the German aggression, a leather document case containing tins of foodstuffs, complete

---

[21] Private N. F., Deposition No. 80.
[22] Lieutenant Colonel G., of Army General Staff, Deposition No. 6.
[23] Second Lieutenant Z., Deposition No. 7.
[24] Lieutenant Colonel G., on Staff of an Army Corps, Deposition No. 10.
[25] Infantry Lieutenant K., attached to Divisional General Staff, Deposition No. 350.

with the commercial labels, was discovered on the edge of a military training ground at Kalisz. The tins were filled with explosive materials and were provided with an opening for the insertion of fuses. I was informed at the staff of the Army Corps to which I was attached that tins of this kind had also been found in other localities."

From an engineer in Łódź:[26]

"During the last days of August rifles, automatic weapons, hand-grenades, and large quantities of ammunition were found at Łódź, Aleksandrów, Konstantynów, and Tomaszów. A secret wireless receiving and transmitting set was also found.

"During the evacuation of the Polish population from the frontier districts, and also from the town of Łódź, the German rural population not only fired at and mishandled civilian evacuees, but even attacked military detachments."

From a Captain in the Polish Calvary:[27]

"The men who had been entrusted with the role of subversive agents knew Polish well and were well informed as to elements favourable to the Reich."

From a member of the Tenth Infantry Regiment:[28]

"Our regiment, after a furious struggle, was surrounded by larger German forces, and surrendered. I decided to get away before being taken prisoner. I succeeded once, but, exhausted by the flight and the necessity to hide in the forest, I was taken by the Germans a second time close to Sochaczew. As I speak German, a gendarme fell into conversation with me and advised me to join the German police. I did not reject this 'offer' out of hand, as I wanted to enjoy the greatest possible liberty of movement. My manoeuvre succeeded. I was no longer kept under supervision. One day as I was seated in the courtyard before the gendarme post, thinking out a plan for escape, a car filled with assault troops in uniform suddenly drove in. One of them who appeared to be their commander spoke to my

---

[26] Engineer Ch., from Łódź, Deposition No. 102.
[27] Cavalry Captain R., Deposition No. 43.
[28] I. R., Tenth Infantry Regiment, Deposition No. 21.

gendarme, then came up to me and said in very good Polish: 'Greetings, M. Lieutenant.' I replied: 'Good day.' He fell into conversation with me, always in Polish, discussing Poland's military defeat and trying to persuade me that Poland's fate was definitely settled. After a time I asked him where he had acquired his perfect knowledge of Polish. He laughed and frankly admitted that he was a German, but of Polish citizenship, that he had been born in Poland and, finally, he had studied at the Polytechnic in Lwów."

From a Polish Sub-lieutenant:[29]
"At Leszno the German population who were Polish citizens (Volksdeutsche) had made preparations in advance to start diversionist activities, and possessed such arms as machine-guns, revolvers, and grenades. Certain Germans, as Dr. Schneider, Veigt, Hausler, and others, fired on the Polish troops and population even before the Polish Army began to retreat, which was on September 3rd, 1939. Veigt, Hausler, and another German whose name I have forgotten, were caught in the act and shot. Many others, Dr. Schneider, for instance, were not disturbed, though they also had fired."

From a Polish Corporal:[30]
"In the district of Krotoszyn, from which I come, the majority of the Germans were secretly organized. They began diversionist activities from the very outbreak of the war. I was not called up for army service, and during those first few days I was able to observe what was happening in my neighbourhood. The son of a very rich German agriculturist, a Polish citizen, named Hermann (of Ochlo village) was the chief agitator among these people. Orders relating to espionage came from his house. When military operations came to an end I returned to the district for a time, and learned that my suspicions and those of my neighbours had been justified. As a reward for services rendered Hermann was appointed administrator of the Bielawa estate and of several others also. Of course he is persecuting the Poles."

---

[29] Sub-lieutenant T. T., Deposition No. 9.
[30] Corporal S. Z., Deposition No. 2.

From a Polish officer on the Army Staff:[31]

"During the month of August, 1939, numerous German officers in civilian dress and furnished with passports arrived in Poland. For instance, several dozens of these men arrived in the province of Pomorze. They had been instructed to familiarize themselves with the Polish terrain and to organize subversive activities among the German colonists and members of German organizations.

"The examination of an agent arrested close to Dębica elicited that the Polish territory was covered with German posts directing and controlling the agents' activities and forming bases of action for them."

From a Lieutenant Colonel on the Polish Army Staff:[32]

"It is beyond all doubt that the German subversive activity in Pomorze was prepared long in advance, both in regard to the selection of agents, their preparation and training, and in regard to their equipment and the detailing of their plan of campaign. The local organizations of the Deutsche Vereinigung and other German organizations served as bases for their subversive activity. In several instances that I have been able to verify, this activity was directed by the Lutheran pastor of the district.

"It was frequently verified in Pomorze that the directors of this activity had been recruited from among Germans who had gone to Germany during the period from March to August, 1939. From the first day of the war they were transported in cars to the rear of the Polish Armies, to the districts they had originated from, where they were put in charge of the subversive activity."

From a Polish Major:[33]

"Shortly before the war a certain number of young German suspects arrived in the German minority villages of the district in which our brigade was stationed. These persons devoted themselves to subversive activity (villages of Konstantynów and Henryków, in the neighbourhood of Częstochowa)."

---

[31] Lieutenant Colonel G., attached to Army Staff, Deposition No. 305.
[32] Lieutenant Colonel R., of Army Staff, 2nd Bureau, Deposition No. 89.
[33] Major L., Deposition No. 310.

From a Polish Lieutenant:[34]

"The espionage and subversive activities were directed by the German organizations Deutsche Vereinigung and Jungdeutsche Partei, whose members had gone illegally to Germany, to the region of Riesengebirge. They there participated in a course lasting two weeks and directed by German officers. They were given instruction in the handling of dynamite, the construction of time bombs, and pistol practice. The organization which I knew was divided into groups of five. At its head were men named Jan Fimmel and Köpfchen-Pawlowski, also the latter's wife. Wolff, the German minority deputy to the Sejm, was one of the creators of this organization."

From a Polish Lieutenant:[35]

"A little time before war broke out, in the course of liquidating subversive activity and espionage in the town of Łódź, twenty-four persons were arrested. They confessed to having made preparations for subversive activities. At the signal, to be sent out from the Breslau broadcasting station, Die Kameraden von Dr. Eichholz zur Arbeit (Comrades of Dr. Eichholz, to work), they were to blow up railway tracks, bridges, and military objectives, of course according to a plan drawn up beforehand, and were to attempt to master the Łódź Central Post Office and telephone exchange. Forty-five kilogrammes of dynamite were discovered, hidden in food tins bearing the label of the Polish Pudliszki factory, and also in double-bottomed bidons of oil. There were also several dozen 'Walter'-type revolvers, clock mechanism for bombs, and wireless receiving apparatus of German make. The arrest of the members of this organization occurred in consequence of a code telegram to the leaders, sent from Germany on August 25th, 1939, and reading: 'Mother dead, buy wreaths.' Thanks to these timely arrests the acts of sabotage and terrorism which the Germans had planned in the Łódź district did not take place."

---

[34] Lieutenant of Infantry, B., Deposition No. 343.
[35] Lieutenant of Infantry, B., attached to General Staff of 10th Army Corps, Deposition No. 377.

From a Polish Second Lieutenant:[36]

"I have not seen one village in the district of Augustów, of Suwałki, or the districts of Białystok province situated close to the German frontier, which did not contain two or three German colonists. Even superficial observation was sufficient to determine that these colonists were working for the German 2nd Bureau. The German youth were especially outstanding in this activity."

Methods of Carrying Out Activity

As has already been mentioned, the German agents were transferred to Poland in the following ways. Immediately before the war they made their way into the territory to which they were assigned, furnished with passports in good order. (In the event this applied principally to the organizers of subversive activity.) At the moment of opening of hostilities they were carried in aeroplanes or cars. This latter method was rendered much easier by the mass exodus of the civil population, among whom they were able to move without difficulty. A certain number of agents penetrated into Poland in this way after the Polish front had been broken by the German motorized units which preceded the army.

Depositions from two Polish officers:[37]

"It would appear from information which we possessed even at the time that parachute descents played a leading part in the German subversive activity in Poland. The parachutists generally descended in the evening, less often at night, and rarely in the daytime also, even while bombs were being dropped...

"The most numerous groups of subversive agents consisted of parachutists, who were joined by civilians, members of the German minority. The number of parachutists dropped at any one time varied from a few to fifteen."

---

[36] Second Lieutenant of Cavalry, D., Deposition No. 11.
[37] Depositions of Lieutenant Colonel C. and Second Lieutenant S.

From a Polish Colonel:[38]

"Diversionist activity was carried out with the aid of the local German colonists. This element, as I was able to ascertain in the course of operations, provided the German air force with the following information:

    a. "It indicated the position of our troops, and in particular the artillery command.

    b. "It informed of our military objectives.

    c. "It reported on the movements of our troops.

"This information was communicated by agreed signs (I found one such sign in the district of Zielonek), by setting fire to various objects (a method largely used to indicate the absence of Polish troops), light signals, and also by wireless apparatus.

"This activity was carried out principally in the rear of our troops. Its primary object was to provoke panic. Such panic was provoked in the rear of the 8th Infantry Division during the night of September 3/4th, in the district of Szulmierz."

From a private citizen:[39]

"I lived at Brześć on the river Bug and I was a carpenter by trade. As Brześć was being subjected to intense bombing from the air I sought refuge in a colony hidden in the Bronna Gora forest. One day, I do not remember the date exactly, we saw, as usual, two German aeroplanes flying at a great height. We noticed that two great parcels appeared to fall from one of them and, a moment later, we saw two parachutes open. We realized that two spies had been dropped, and five men from our colony, armed with whatever came to hand—a forester in particular had a gun— ran towards where the parachutes were dropping. The airmen obviously had not noticed our colony, and had dropped their passengers quite close to the spot where we were watching. We managed to capture them and discovered that they had no documents whatever on them, that they were dressed in civilian clothes, but wore a kind of brassard on the sleeve of their shirt, under the jacket. They were armed with revolvers, which we handed to the police at Bereza Kartuska. In addition each of them had two

---

[38] Colonel S., Deposition No. 425.

[39] M. Jean S., Deposition No. 71.

small hand-grenades, they carried wire-cutters, and one of them had three small phials filled with a liquid."

From a Polish Colonel:[40]

"In the vicinity of Rzeszów, close to Lwów, a woman who descended by parachute was arrested. She was a German colonist from a neighbouring village, and it was suspected that she had not been at home for fifteen days.

"The majority of the parachutists were provided with explosives. They descended principally in the vicinity of the objects they were to blow up. A large number of them were discovered on the banks of the rivers Dunajec, Vistula, and Wisłoka."

From a Polish Calvary Captain:[41]

"The Germans practised their subversive activities with extraordinary skill. Far in the rear of our armies they had marked out districts where aeroplanes transporting agents made landings. (I myself saw aeroplanes land in the Garwolin-Dęblin sector.) The motorized columns of the German Army made towards these regions.

"Thus, in our rear or in the vicinity, the Germans got control of our principal lines of communication from the bases, so that the subversive activity could develop efficaciously."

From a Polish Major:[42]

"The German information service made use of agents and also, for espionage purposes, of German colonists. Parachutists were dropped in the vicinity of minority settlements, who put them up, facilitated their task, and concealed them."

---

[40] Colonel G., Deposition No. 500.
[41] Cavalry Captain R., Deposition No. 494.
[42] Infantry Major W., Deposition No. 450.

From a Polish Reserve Lieutenant:[43]

"On our road we encountered agents, descended by parachute, who were arrested by the police and the civilian population. Fourteen such were arrested in the vicinity of uncut."

From a Polish Lieutenant:[44]

"The subversive agents dropped by parachute at once mixed with the refugees. Thus it was very difficult to discover them."

From a Polish Major:[45]

"Between September 15th and 16th, in the vicinity of Garwolin, I discovered a group of German agents armed with rifles and small machine-guns, who opened fire on my detachment. The night was falling. I managed to surround them and took prisoner eighty-six persons in civilian clothes, carrying arms. Ten of them were Germans from the Reich, who had descended by parachute; the others were Germans from the district of Garwolin.

"During the following days I ascertained the presence of a large number of agents trying to provoke panic in the rear, for example, by setting fire to haystacks, and also to villages."

From a Polish Lieutenant of Artillery:[46]

"I personally saw two individuals who had descended by parachute some fifteen kilometres from the town of Kraśnik, who had been arrested by the local civilian population. One of them had not had time to get free of his parachute; both of them came from Silesia originally."

From a Polish Captain attached to Brigade Staff:[47]

"I myself saw two parachutists descend, equipped with a wireless transmitter."

---

[43] Reserve Lieutenant M., Deposition No. 104.

[44] Lieutenant P., Deposition No. 18.

[45] Major M., Deposition No. 87.

[46] Lieutenant of Artillery, Battery Commander K., Deposition No. 39.

[47] Captain S., attached to a Brigade Staff, Deposition No. 12.

From another Polish Captain:[48]

"On September 4th, 1939, several aeroplanes dropped six men provided with bicycles and automatic pistols in the neighbourhood of Czerwony Bor."

The subversive agents were disguised both in military uniform (as officers, non-commissioned officers, and privates) and in civilian clothes (as workmen, beggars, priests, members of religious orders, etc.).

Independently of the extended network of shortwave wireless transmitting stations which had been installed before the war broke out, mainly in western Poland, the parachutists were provided with small transmitting and receiving sets. In addition they were provided with bicycles, automatic pistols, rocket-pistols, electric lamps, and explosives.

From a Polish Captain:[49]

"At six in the morning of September 6th Germans dressed as Polish non-commissioned officers and provided with Polish documents were found near Wielki Radomyśl. They also had a suitcase containing explosive materials.

"The same evening a car carrying four persons, one of them a woman, was met with at Wielki Radomyśl. They were wearing Polish military greatcoats. As appeared later, these Polish greatcoats covered German uniforms. One of them was betrayed by the collar of his German uniform which showed above his greatcoat. They were arrested by Reserve Lieutenant I.

"Diversionist agents descended by aeroplane in the neighbourhood of Biłgoraj. They were armed with revolvers and hand-grenades. They were arrested and handed over to the military authorities."

From a Polish Second Lieutenant:[50]

"Diversionist activity was organized by the German minority. Its agents were distinguished by yellow collars, piping, buttons of distinctive shape, pullovers, etc."

---

[48] Captain M., Deposition No. 497
[49] Captain G., Deposition No. 280.
[50] Second Lieutenant T. S., Light Artillery, Deposition No. 185.

From a Polish Calvary Captain:[51]

"The subversive agents were frequently disguised as soldiers, recruits, etc., of the Polish Army. They were distinguished by some peculiarity in their dress, by a band, a muffler, etc."

From a Polish Reserve Second Lieutenant:[52]

"In the district of Łomża a large number of subversive agents disguised as women or priests were arrested. There was general co-operation between the German minority and these agents."

From a Polish Captain of the Artillery:[53]

"The numerous diversionist agents who were captured, and who were almost always shot on the spot, were recruited mainly from among people who during the first day of Polish evacuation from Upper Silesia filtered in among the crowd of refugees. At first they were only civilians; later on diversionist agents dressed in Polish uniforms were captured.

"On September 9th, 1939, the Germans sent diversionist agents wearing the Nazi brassard into Stopnica in two lorries. This band tore at full speed into the market-place at Stopnica and there dispersed into various houses, then threw a rain of hand-grenades into the neighbouring streets. This band was soon completely wiped out."

From a Polish Calvary Lieutenant:[54]

"While making a fighting retreat in the direction of Radomyśl we were attacked by a group of some thirty diversionist agents. Hidden in the undergrowth, they were observing our operations. When attacked by our soldiers they fled into the forest. Two of them were killed. They were dressed in Polish uniform, armed with German Mausers, and light machine-guns of type No. 34, and had small electric lamps with white, red, and green bulbs. No papers whatever were found on them. The local civilian population testified that these agents had descended by parachute about eight o'clock in the evening and immediately after sent up red

---

[51] Cavalry Captain R., attached to a Brigade Staff, Deposition No. 393.
[52] Reserve Second Lieutenant R., Deposition No. 134.
[53] Captain of Artillery, L. F., Deposition No. 236.
[54] Cavalry Lieutenant I. A., 2nd Light Cavalry Regiment, Deposition No. 392.

signals. *During air raids on Tarnów on September 4th, 1939, the airmen bombed objectives lit up with powerful electric lamps by spies on the ground. One of the spies was captured in the uniform of a Polish Lieutenant. In the course of the operations the diversionist agents made especial use of red, green, and white electric light signals. When they landed the agents made signals with little luminous red balls which burst after ten to fifteen seconds."*

From a Polish Major:[55]

"On September 2nd, 1939, at about 11 a.m., two individuals wearing Polish non-commissioned officers' uniform arrived on motorbicycles of Polish manufacture at the village of Bukowno, in Olkusz district. They went up to a refugee from German Silesia and, after exchanging a few words with him, shot him with a revolver. The inquiry made on the spot elicited that the victim was an organizer of the Polish population in German Silesia and a fervent Polish patriot, while the assassins were Germans disguised as Polish non-commissioned officers."

From a Captain attached to the staff of an operational group:[56]

"Returning during the night of September loth from Ossowiec in the direction of Wysokie Mazowieckie, I noticed a car halted on the road, and in it three officers armed with rifles. They informed me that they belonged to an independently acting cavalry brigade and were going to Białystok, carrying special orders. I asked them about the situation, they answered that it had not changed at all and that I could continue my journey 'in full security.' In reality the town of Wysokie Mazowieckie was already on fire, and the German tanks were operating in the immediate neighbourhood. When I had gone some two hundred metres I heard a rifle-shot fired in my direction."

From a Polish Captain of a Chasseurs Regiment:[57]

"On September 6th, 1939, two German spies in civilian dress were arrested at the edge of a wood some three kilometres from Tomaszów.

---

[55] Dr. G., Major, Deposition No. 107.
[56] Captain M., attached to the staff of an operational group, Deposition No. 110.
[57] Captain T. S., 45th Chasseurs Regiment, Deposition No. 334.

They admitted that they were German colonists and had orders to pass themselves off as Polish soldiers evading German capture, taken prisoner, and now in flight, with the object of getting information about the disposition of Polish troops and informing the Germans."

From a Polish Infantry Major:[58]
"The agents dropped from aeroplanes were provided with rocket-pistols, and, by firing rockets of agreed colours, caused either artillery or aerial bombardments."

From a Polish Lieutenant attached to the staff of an Infantry Division:[59]
"Air raids took place in the Poznań areas during the 1st and 2nd September. One aeroplane came down and two German airmen were taken prisoner. The German Second Lieutenant came from Stargard in German Pomerania, and carried instructions and badges for German diversionist agents.

"During the night of September 1st civilian detachments (Freikorps) attacked the town of Ujście and massacred the Polish population, including women and children. Two spies carrying secret wireless transmitting sets were arrested.

"The German civilian population attempted to combat our reconnaissance elements, which effectively dealt with this attempt.

"On September 1st in the district of Stryków we established the fact of the participation of civilians of the German minority, armed with rifles and pistols, in the action (massacring our prisoners). (Reported by a private of the 57th infantry regiment, who was taken prisoner in the woods, but escaped.)"

From a Polish Lieutenant of an artillery Regiment:[60]
"The information transmitted by wireless transmitting and receiving sets were decoded mainly by the aid of an agreed key. House chimneys were painted white; at night these chimneys were coloured with various

[58] Infantry Major W., Deposition No. 29.
[59] Lieutenant Z. Z., attached to staff of Infantry Division 14, Deposition No. 288.
[60] Lieutenant Z., 1st Artillery Regiment, Deposition No. 410.

colours in accordance with the agreed signal code. Objectives for bombardment were also indicated by rockets. The diversionist agents wore the uniforms of our officers, passed themselves off as liaison officers of the high command, and issued orders in its name. They passed themselves off as wounded and got themselves evacuated to the interior of the country. They had secret documents hidden under their false bandages. In the mountains the fire of the enemy artillery was directed by rockets from spies hidden on the summits. Diversionist agents, disguised in Polish officers' and soldiers' uniforms, and also in civilian dress, descended in aeroplanes."

From a Polish Lieutenant in a Regiment of Lancers:[61]

"There were parachutists in the forests. Despite all our efforts, their capture proved very difficult. But the local population helped a great deal. Thus, on September 6th, close to Łupkowo, as the result of information supplied by two shepherd lads, my lancers arrested two parachutist diversionist agents. They spoke Polish. I handed them over to my superior military authorities. Spies swarmed everywhere. One fact from many: Close to Łupków a German owner of a brickyard possessed a transmitting set and, moreover, indicated the direction of the wind to German airmen, from his yard. He was executed on September 6th.

"Parachutists: On September 7th our lancers captured two parachutist diversionist agents in a clearing close to the Ryszki estate. They carried revolvers and explosive materials."

From a Polish Sub-lieutenant:[62]

"In the forest near Tomaszów we discovered two German wireless transmitting posts in a dug-out."

From another Polish Sub-lieutenant:[63]

"At Buznie I arrested the pastor Blümel and his son who were inculpated in diversionist activities, and handed them over to our State Military Police. I discovered proofs of the existence of a wireless transmitter

---

[61] Lieutenant S., 27th Regiment of Lancers, Deposition No. 352.
[62] Sub-lieutenant R. T., Deposition No. 499.
[63] Sub-lieutenant N. 0., Deposition No. 273.

and also three typewriters for writing pamphlets which were hidden under the altar of the Protestant church."

From a Lieutenant Colonel of the Polish Army General Staff:[64]
"The network of short-wave transmitter stations established by the German spies was so well arranged and the stations themselves so cleverly hidden that they were discovered only by chance. For instance, such stations were found in the tomb of a well-known industrialist at Poznań, in the house of a Protestant pastor at Luck, and in a hollow tree in a forest near Kowalewo in Pomorze."

From another Lieutenant Colonel of the Polish Army General Staff:[65]
"In the course of domiciliary visits to Germans made between September 1st and 7th, in the Pomorze province, fifteen short-wave transmission stations were discovered."

From a Polish Sub-lieutenant:[66]
"On September 6th, 1939, the command of the Gdynia defence came into possession of a short-wave transmitter set dropped by parachute from an aeroplane and found not far from a farm which belonged to a minority German of Polish citizenship."

From a Polish Infantry Captain:[67]
"On September 7th or 8th Lieutenant B. Z., now dead, of the 42nd Infantry Regiment, informed me that a short-wave station was said to have been installed in the tower of the Protestant church at Białystok. He said that the pastor communicated with the enemy by means of this set.

"On September 16th or 17th I was in Białystok when a German attack was made in the direction of the Central Railway Station. I myself heard revolver shots fired on the boulevard, in Piast Street, where I happened to be at the time. The firing caused a panic in this part of the

---

[64] Lieutenant Colonel G., attached to Army General Staff, Deposition No. 203.
[65] Lieutenant Colonel R., attached to Army General Staff, Deposition No. 24.
[66] Sub-lieutenant J., Deposition No.25.
[67] Captain A. E., 42nd Infantry Regiment, Deposition No. 412.

town, which was on the farther side of the town from the actual hostilities. It was German agents trying to make a diversion.

"On September 23rd, 1939, I was at Sejny. Here I heard that a student of the college at Sejny had been shot down piloting an aeroplane near Suwałki. This student admitted that he had been assigned the task of bombing Sejny. To establish his identity, the professor of his class was summoned to Suwałki, and recognized him at once."

From a Polish Artillery Captain:[68]

"From personal observation I was able to confirm that the Germans enrolled representatives of intellectuals, workers, and farmer classes for their espionage service. I learned from an eye-witness who arrested a forester named Muller at Biłgoraj that this man possessed a small short-wave set and a large number of photographs, which he sent to Berlin. Also through the wireless set diversionist agents communicated with German airmen. The diversionist agents were always in the uniform either of Polish soldiers or of Polish police."

From a Polish platoon commander:[69]

"Wherever the German troops advanced there were settlements of German colonists. (The houses of these colonists were distinguished by white crosses painted on the roofs.) In the forest close to Żychlin (Kutno) our wireless telegraphists discovered a shelter where a German wireless station had been installed for some long time. The aerial was hidden in one of the trees."

Ground Signals Made to Airmen

From a Polish pilot:[70]

"I knew our camouflaged aerodrome at Werynia very well. It was some miles from the San. Imagine my astonishment when, coming down one day, when still some distance away I saw great white signs which had not been there before. I was uncertain whether to land or not. When I

---

[68] Artillery Captain Ch., Deposition No. 339.
[69] Temporary Officer B. P., Platoon Commander, 60th Infantry Regiment, Deposition No. 468.
[70] Pilot Second Lieutenant M. Z., Deposition No. 115.

did land, I immediately ascertained the origin of these signs. A hurried inquiry revealed that they were the work of local Germans. Unfortunately, the culprits had fled, and we had no time to go in pursuit of the spies."

From a Polish Captain, a pilot observer:[71]

"In the vicinity of Luck diversionist agents were dropped by parachute at night. These agents (among whom were women) lived in neighbouring German villages; they were provided with Polish documents in good order and evoked no suspicions whatever. Among other tasks they were to make agreed signals on the ground for advising the German airmen.

"These signals were made in various ways:

    d. *"The grass in a field was mowed according to a plan.*

    e. *"Ricks were stacked in special arrangements in a field.*

    f. *"A ploughed field was trodden down according to a plan.*

"I have seen photographs taken of these signals; some of them had the following forms:"

Illustrations of Signals Made by Germans Living in Poland to Direct German Pilots to their Targets

From a Polish Infantry Sub-lieutenant:[72]

"On September 7th, 1939, I caught a German diversionist agent cutting wires in the Praga suburb of Warsaw. On searching his house I found weapons and maps. In another German house I found apparatus for making light signals."

---

[71] Captain S. K., Pilot Observer, Deposition No. 257.
[72] Infantry Sub-lieutenant A. F., Deposition No. 404.

From a Polish Captain of the Police Inquiry Board at Puck:[73]

"The following were the signs agreed between the German airmen and diversionist agents during the Polish-German war.

1. Designs made by treading down tilled ground.

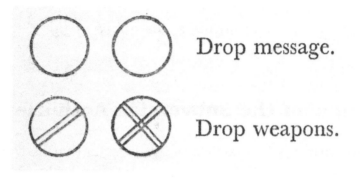

Drop message.

Drop weapons.

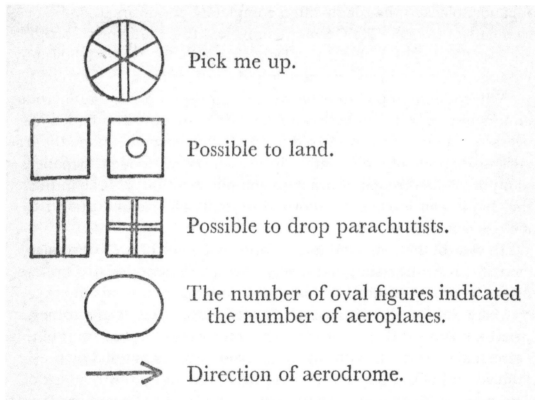

Pick me up.

Possible to land.

Possible to drop parachutists.

The number of oval figures indicated the number of aeroplanes.

Direction of aerodrome.

[73] Captain W. K., Police Inquiry Board at Puck, Deposition No. 413.

2. By the disposition of hay and corn stooks.

3. By scything grain according to the above designs.
4. By painting the roofs.
5. By light signals (rockets or lights in chimneys).

Aims of the Subversive Activities

One of the principal purposes of all these activities was the spreading of panic among the civilian population which, in tens of thousands, blocked the roads, often completely paralysing the movements of troops. The Germans provoked this panic by resort to terror (see Lieutenant Colonel R.'s Deposition No. 24, which follows) by circulating alarming news and starting incendiary fires.

While military operations were in progress there were numerous instances of engagements between Polish detachments and bands of subversive agents. These occurred most of all in Pomorze; none the less, in various districts of the country civilians carrying no identity papers fired on the Polish troops. It must be emphasized that, just as in the case of the German air force and motorized units, the German authorities made use primarily of the very young.

In view of the thorough nature and vast scale of the subversive activity it is not surprising that a very natural reaction led to a no less dangerous state of mind which saw spies and subversive agents everywhere. This state was also manifested among the Polish armies, and it must be assumed that the Germans foresaw and took account of this circumstance. For that matter it was considerably facilitated by the circumstances of the German-Polish war, and above all by the lack of liaison between the various detachments which were disorganized by the aggression of the German air force, the inadequate activity of the wireless, the lack of newspapers, the evacuation of the civil authorities, etc.

The subversive activities carried out by German agents in the rear of the Polish armies had for object:

1. To collaborate actively with the air force, to indicate bombing objectives to it.

2. To destroy lines of communication (cutting telegraph and telephone wires, destroying railways, damaging bridges, etc.).

3. To attack military transports.

4. To destroy public utilities services.

Deposition from Lieutenant Colonel R.:[74]

"One of the principal objects of the German agents was to spread panic among the civilian population, following a method which was observable in numerous cases registered in the districts of Wyrzysk and Sempolno, in the south-western part of Pomorze.

"Immediately the Germans marched into a Polish locality they arrested all the men, and forced the women and children to take to flight, informing them that all the men would be shot.

"These women and children fled farther east, towards the centre of the country, and carried with them the population of the districts through which they passed. The crowds increased rapidly, blocking all the roads and obstructing the movements of troops."

From a Lieutenant Colonel attached to the Polish Army General Staff:[75]

"During the fighting close to Cracow the civilian population took to flight eastward, incited by minority agents.

"Rumours circulated among the regiments that the orders given had been revoked, and that they had been advised to throw down their arms.

"When the Polish regiments found themselves obliged to cross the Hungarian frontier German agents persuaded the soldiers that their higher commands had ordered them to abandon their arms."

---

[74] Lieutenant Colonel R., attached to Army General Staff, Deposition No. 24.
[75] Lieutenant Colonel S., attached to Army General Staff, Deposition No. 59.

From a Polish Lieutenant:[76]

"I became certain that, before the German motorized columns undertook any action of any large dimensions, rumours were put into circulation by their agents in our rear that the German tanks had already reached this or that locality. These rumours did not correspond in the least to the reality. These agents were regularly concealed by the German colonists."

From a Sub-lieutenant in the Polish Artillery:[77]

"False news spread for the purpose of provoking panic was the order of the day. The German agents in Pomorze disorganized the military transports by attacking them with machine-guns, while others, disguised as Polish soldiers, gave the signal for flight, as the result of which the road was swiftly blocked by lorries, wagons, etc. Frequently the German airmen took the opportunity to machine-gun the transports by flying low over them.

Subversive agents, frequently disguised as Polish officers or soldiers, distributed leaflets urging the soldiers to mutiny against their officers. Two agents were captured close to Solec Kujawski while attempting to destroy telephone cables. On one of them anti-Polish leaflets were found."

From a Lieutenant attached to a Divisional Staff in the Polish Infantry:[78]

"In order to demoralize the Polish troops the Germans scattered leaflets which read more or less as follows: 'The Polish Army is broken up, all Poland is in German occupation. To obtain an honourable peace arms must be laid down immediately. The Polish soldiers fighting in the rear of the German armies will be treated as ordinary bandits and shot. The Germans are bringing order and peace with them, they intend to spare the Polish self-respect. When the German troops entered Cracow the German command made a point of setting a guard of honour over Marshal

---

[76] Lieutenant C., Deposition No. 83.
[77] Sub-lieutenant of Artillery, H., Deposition No. 87.
[78] Infantry Lieutenant B., attached to a Divisional Staff, Deposition No. 14.

Piłsudski's tomb. You must surrender at once! In that case all the Polish soldiers will be treated well.'

"'Warsaw has fallen,' was proclaimed in leaflets from September 13th onward, and the Breslau wireless station, broadcasting on the Warsaw station's wavelengths, repeated the statement."

From a Polish Infantry Sub-lieutenant:[79]

"I was in Bydgoszcz on September 3rd, 1939, while Polish troops were still in the town. I was witness of the following scene: about ten in the morning several minority Germans who spoke Polish well, so far as a hurried examination enabled one to determine, rushed into the street, shouting that the German armies had already entered the town and were already in its suburbs. The transports were seized with panic and took to flight. I was on duty in the centre of the town, and, accompanied by police authorities, at once made in a car for the Inowroclaw road, where, aided by several other officers, I managed to halt the flight. The force stationed in the town withstood a fusillade from the German organized elements, and a regular battle took place in the streets."

From a Polish Calvary Lieutenant:[80]

"On September 1st, 1939, I read a German leaflet, according to which any Polish soldiers fighting in the rear of the German Army and captured with arms in hand would not enjoy combatants' rights, but would be treated and punished as francs-tireurs. The leaflet was in two languages, Polish and German."

From a Second Lieutenant in the Polish Infantry:[81]

"The German infantry employed certain signals used by the Polish Army, such as 'cease fire.' This caused considerable confusion among our regiments, especially if fighting was taking place at night."

---

[79] Infantry Sub-lieutenant B., Deposition No. 108.
[80] Cavalry Lieutenant Z., Deposition No. 414.
[81] Second Lieutenant of Infantry, B., Deposition No. 213.

From a Polish Cavalry Lieutenant:[82]

"The German aeroplanes scattered leaflets which said, inter alia: 'Soldiers, you are fighting like lions, but your sacrifice will be in vain, you are lost! Cease fighting.' Appeals of this kind were also made by wireless. The German spies and subversive agents knew Polish very well. In addition their directors were provided with Polish-German vocabularies."

From a Polish Major:[83]

"The detachments of subversive agents were perfectly acquainted with the terrain, and developed their activity immediately in the rear of the combatant armies by attacking not only transports but also isolated detachments of infantry, batteries, etc.

"In one district a priest told me that when the Germans took Sochaczew on September 6th and 7th, they consisted of only six hundred men, infantry, tanks, and artillery. But they were followed by a thousand Germans dressed in Polish uniforms. In addition ninety-five German peasants of Polish citizenship were captured, carrying bundles containing various articles which they had pillaged. The majority of them had Polish mobilization orders calling them to their regiments in Pomorze and Poznańia, and dated between August 14th and 28th, 1939. All except one were Protestants, and they were wretchedly clothed. They were judged guilty of pillage and desertion. Others had German staff maps on the scale of 1:100,000. When examining the papers of another group of Germans, I found three words written in pencil: 'Trojanowski, Sanki, Gąbin.' The meaning of this was found to be: 'Inform the German General Staff at Trojanowski mill that the Polish staff is being transferred by night from Sanki to Gąbin.' Of course, the Polish staff remained at Sanki, but Gąbin was bombarded the next day."

From a Polish Lieutenant in a Cavalry Brigade:[84]

"When the war broke out my detachment was in the district of Lubna, situated some six kilometres from Czersk and about twenty kilometres from Chojnice.

---

[82] Cavalry Lieutenant W., Deposition No. 214.
[83] Major (Dr.) J., Deposition No. 203,
[84] Lieutenant G. D., Pomorze Cavalry Brigade, Deposition No. 69.

"The Germans began the war with a diversionist action. On September 1st, before dawn, the German frontier railway station sent a telephonogram to the station at Chojnice, to ask that two passenger trains alleged to be taking Poles sent from Germany back to their own country should be allowed to pass through. Transit traffic being a normal operation on this line, the ruse succeeded, and Chojnice gave the order for the said trains to be allowed through. But instead of the passenger trains advised, an armoured train arrived, preceded by a railway light car, also armoured, to which (a characteristic detail) a Polish flag had been fixed.

"The armoured train immediately opened fire on the town with its guns, while the light car was engaged farther into our territory and was only demolished there. I assisted at the examination of the men it was carrying. Of course none of them could say how it happened that they had made treacherous use of the Polish flag. But our soldiers had realized that they were faced with German troops only when the latter opened fire on them.

"The diversion activities practised by the German colonists began during the night of September 1st/2nd. In Pomorze they were favoured by wooded districts and by the difficult terrain, which enabled the local population to orientate well and to hide. That very night we saw coloured rockets bursting again and again, indicating the disposition of our troops to the enemy army. All the time we were at the front we could see rockets wherever there were German colonists in the vicinity, and not only in Pomorze, but also close to Włocławek and Ciechocinek. Several times we were able to arrest the men carrying out diversionist activity, and each time we found them in possession of German-made cartridges for rocket-firing. They were always colonists established in Poland.

"In addition to rockets, the German diversionists also had another method of indicating by night the route and the direction our troops were taking. Objects situated close to the route were set on fire without good reason, and always in such a manner as to indicate the beginning of our column. The fire was lighted before the arrival of our troops, and we were never able to lay our hands on the incendiaries. The local Polish population informed us that they were armed men assigned to diversionist activities.

At night the line of burning objects even better revealed the line of our route and our roads.

"On September 4th our detachment was transferred to Łęgnowo, close to Brdyujście, in the neighbourhood of Bydgoszcz. I must mention that at that time this district was still a great distance from the front line. At Łęgnowo, where there was a large number of German colonists, diversionist activities took on very considerable proportions. Thus, during billeting operations my corporal, Grodecki, and another of my subordinates were fired at from rifles when they entered houses. In the same district a considerable store of picks, spades, and wire-cutters, some six hundred items altogether, was found in the Protestant church. They were implements collected in readiness for the demolition of the nearby line of defence. The pastor had fled to Germany on the eve of the war. In this same Łęgnowo we were attacked by a diversionist band, and firing lasted an hour.

"Afterwards we were stationed at the village of Cierpice. Close to Cierpice is the German village of Nieszawka, consisting of some sixty houses. In this village I found a small short-wave wireless transmitter in a box not much bigger than a matchbox. In the same village we were frequently fired on during the night by Germans. We managed to capture one, who admitted that his band numbered three hundred men, and that during the day they hid on the bank of the River Vistula. At night they fired on the Polish detachments and massacred men who had been outstanding in public activities or were members of Polish societies. In the same village I ascertained that the liaison among the Germans was organized by a system of couriers.

"On September 6th, as we were entering the village of Lubienka, to the north of Toruń, I saw a desperate woman running towards me. She complained that the proprietor of a local restaurant and the miller of Lubienka, both of them Germans, had killed her husband. The man, as I was able to determine for myself, had been simply assassinated. Summing up, I affirm that during all these days our soldiers had not a moment of respite and had to be prepared against sudden aggression at any moment."

From a Polish Second Lieutenant of Artillery:[85]

"Close to Solec Kujawski our battery was attacked by subversive agents who fired on us. After scouring the neighbouring woods we found two agents in civilian dress, members of the German minority. They also had new Polish uniforms."

From a Second Lieutenant in the Polish Infantry:[86]

"I was wounded by German agents at Inowroclaw, which I entered with our battalion's advance-guard. The Germans had taken up positions in buildings along the streets of the town; they were armed with machine-guns."

From a Polish Reserve Sub-lieutenant:[87]

"During my regiment's attack upon Tokary, Rombierz, and Tokary-Mlyny, German subversive agents were hidden so cleverly in the marshes and bogs that our soldiers passed close to them without noticing them. They afterwards attacked our detachments, firing at their backs."

From a Polish Lieutenant Colonel attached to a Divisional General Staff:[88]

"On September 7th, 1939, francs-tireurs fired on the 7th Infantry Regiment which had left Łódź and was passing through the village of Nowosolna, which had a majority of German inhabitants."

From a Sub-lieutenant in the Polish Military Police:[89]

"In the localities of Izabelów and Annopol (close to Zduńska Wola) shots were fired by the German civilian populations against detachments of the 10th Division."

---

[85] Second Lieutenant of Artillery, H., Deposition No. 60.
[86] Infantry Second Lieutenant K., Deposition No. 130.
[87] Reserve Sub-lieutenant C., Deposition No. 131.
[88] Lieutenant Colonel P., attached to a Divisional General Staff, Deposition No. 36.
[89] Sub-lieutenant W., in Military Police, Deposition No. 444.

From another Polish Sub-lieutenant:[90]

"On September 11th, 1939, I was ordered by the General Staff to change my quarters and to go to a spot some two kilometres to the north of Biłgoraj. As the town had been burnt by German spies I could not execute this order."

From a Lieutenant in a Polish Armoured Group:[91]

"On September 7th I was sent with a detachment of three armoured cars and a motor-cycle on a reconnaissance from Toruń along the road leading to Chełmno. The road was deserted, and, after covering some ten kilometres, we reached the village of Wypsz, about a kilometre and half from the Wypczyki estate. When we entered the village we were met by the population who complained and lamented, telling us that a German detachment led by the man who rented the said estate and a dairyman named Nitman —both of them Polish citizens of German nationality and long resident in the district—had arrived in the village that morning. These men pointed out the most active of their Polish neighbours to the German soldiers, and the Poles were shot on the spot. I saw their bodies in the houses."

From a Polish Sub-lieutenant:[92]

"I know an instance of a murder committed by a German spy. The victim, Captain Tadeusz Jakubowski, of the eighth Field Artillery Regiment (attached to the 71st group of heavy artillery), born at Warsaw, and aged 42, was killed by a shot in the back in the evening of September 6th or 7th, at Ciechanowice, near Gostyń. This estate belonged to a German named Keilich."

From Second Lieutenant of the Polish Infantry:[93]

"Civil diversionist activity, especially in the frontier zone, seriously hindered military operations. The moment the enemy crossed the frontier the German civilian population living in villages in the vicinity of Leszno openly appeared with machine-guns. Such incidents occurred, inter alia, at

[90] Sub-lieutenant E. H. N., Deposition No. 207.
[91] Lieutenant W. C., of 81st Armoured Group, Deposition No. 40.
[92] Sub-lieutenant E. R, Deposition No. 433.
[93] Second Lieutenant of Infantry, S. F. C., Deposition No. 467.

the villages of Gronowo and Wloszkowice. It would have been impossible to count the shots fired from carbines and sporting guns. In the neighbourhood of Radzyn diversionist agents punctured with revolver shots two tyres of a lorry transporting troops. The houses occupied by German colonists were left intact. The organization was so good that the German houses were marked on the roofs or by distinctive signs formed of straw placed close to the house. Thus the locality of Aleksandrów, close to Żychlin, and inhabited by a German colony, was unharmed, although all the surrounding villages were devastated."

From a private citizen:[94]

"On September 7th or 8th I was travelling with my wife in a car along the road from Lublin to Lwów. On the road, which otherwise was deserted, I was stopped by a heavy open lorry transporting our troops. The men told me that a few moments before an open car with three civilians in it had passed them, and several grenades had been thrown at them. One of the grenades missed, the second only half exploded, and the men showed it to me: it was of German make. A third wounded two soldiers. I took several men, and we raced in pursuit of the aggressors, but failed to overtake them."

From a Polish Colonel:[95]

"On the right bank of the river Brda at Bydgoszcz is the river sports club of the Postal Military Training Association. A group of postal employees had gathered there on September 3rd, 1939, when suddenly firing broke out. It came from the left bank of the river, where a group of diversionist agents was lying in ambush. The next day, about six in the afternoon, German civilians fired at and killed a liaison officer who was driving along the road in a car, some ten kilometres from Toruń.

"In the afternoon of September 6th I saw two villages deliberately set on fire on the road from Biała Podlaska. There were no troops anywhere in the neighbourhood. Not one soldier in either of the two villages. So the only reason for burning them must have been a desire to destroy and devastate the property of the Polish population."

---

94 E. H., Deposition No. 34.
95 Colonel R. D., Deposition No. 34.

From a Polish Major:[96]

"I certify that I saw the case of Lieutenant Kowalski, who was stationed with me at a colony in Wolhynia, in which there were German inhabitants. He washed himself with water which the mistress of the house brought him in a bowl, and immediately his face swelled up terribly. He was taken at once to the hospital at Luck, where it was diagnosed that his burns were due to mustard gas, fortunately in a diluted form.

"I certify that throughout the campaign in Poland I came across diversionist operations consisting of cutting telephone wires. Also in districts behind the front we were fired on at night, and always where there were German colonies, even in the neighbourhood of Warsaw. I had one characteristic experience: my men informed me that they had seen a peasant ploughing his field in a strange way, tracing zigzags and circles with his plough. After examining the field, I decided that his ploughing had nothing to do with ordinary field labour, and, after tracing on paper the designs he had made, we saw that it was a gigantic figure which he had made for the benefit of enemy airmen."

From a private citizen:[97]

"I had to go to Leszno on business. I certify that I saw German inhabitants firing from their windows at Polish troops in retreat. I assisted to disarm a man named Müller—I do not remember his Christian name. He was an artisan living in Leszno, who had gone to Germany a year before the war broke out. He did not turn up again in Leszno until after the outbreak of hostilities, and then he was armed with a machine-gun."

From a Polish soldier:[98]

"During the early days of the war I was stationed near Solec in Pomorze. Our armoured cars were standing in the open fields quite a long distance from any houses. During the night I noticed a young man, dressed in civilian clothes, who appeared to be looking for something close to our cars. As I had suspicions of him I arrested him. He was a young man, a German colonist from Solec. On searching him I found

---

[96] Major S. F., Deposition No. 70.
[97] F. C., Deposition No. 32.
[98] T. W., Deposition No. 31.

some tow and rag soaked in petrol under his jacket. He was unable to give me any logical explanation of his presence at night near our cars, so far from inhabited houses. His name was Johann Bauman, and from the examination of the man we learned that he had fled to Germany six months before the war. He had come back in order to carry out diversionist activity.

"During the retreat I halted in my native village, Nowy Zbrachlin, in the district of Nieszawa, Warsaw Province. There friends of mine told me, to my great astonishment, that they had surprised two Germans, Karl Bar and Johann Müller, attempting to cut wires. It was surprising because they were the only Germans who had lived in this district for generations, and they had always been regarded as our own people."

From a Second Lieutenant in the Polish Cavalry:[99]

"On September 5th, 1939, in the vicinity of Opoczno I was fired at by a German colonist armed with a revolver, but he missed me. He was killed by an artillery officer mounted on a horse, Lieutenant X."

From another Second Lieutenant in the Polish Calvary:[100]

"Close to Włoki, where the 23rd Infantry Regiment was acting on the defence, a German in civilian dress, perched on a haystack, made signals to the Germans with a small flag during the attack.

"On the banks of the Brda, several Polish soldiers who were cut off were massacred by the German minority civilian population. In the woods close to Solec Kujawski German bands in civilian dress attacked troops of the 23rd Infantry Regiment.

"The German population of Bydgoszcz fired from the windows of their houses at the third battalion of the 23rd Infantry Regiment."

From yet another:[101]

---

[99] Second Lieutenant of Cavalry, J. Z., Deposition No. 88.
[100] Second Lieutenant of Infantry, R., Deposition No. 215.
[101] Second Lieutenant of Infantry, J., Deposition No. 210.

"A transport of wounded which was travelling in a motor bus was twice attacked during the night of September 10th/11th, 1939, close to Siedlce, by German bands of agents. Some of the agents were shot by unwounded and less seriously wounded soldiers."

And from yet another:[102]

"Subversive agents fired on the regiments in retreat and on trains transporting evacuated civilians. They impeded road traffic by felling trees (at Olkusz), they fired on officers (at Trzebinia). They were often disguised as military police or as Polish railway officials. At Rabsztyn an agent was disguised as a Polish Sub-lieutenant. Their German documents were concealed in the lining of their clothes. They were armed with carbines, revolvers, and grenades.

"They operated at night for preference, setting fire to villages, attacking the defenceless civilian population, and sowing panic as the Polish armies retreated."

From a doctor attached to the Polish Army Staff:[103]

"I was attached to the staff of General Bortnowski's army. During the campaign I myself witnessed or received precise information of the following incidents of a subversive nature.

"At Toruń, thirty-four persons were shot who had been caught in the act of making signals with mirrors or white material during attacks by German bombers.

"While on my way from Włocławek to Ciechocinek to give the necessary instructions for the evacuation of the military hospital, I met police officers escorting a group of diversionist agents, twenty-three persons altogether, including three women. From what they said it appeared that they had been captured with weapons in their hands. The police officers asked what they were to do, as the men lay down on the ground and refused to go on. I told them they must carry out their orders, which were to conduct the Germans before the requisite authorities.

---

[102] Second Lieutenant of Infantry, Platoon Commander, Deposition No. 316.
[103] Dr. J. B., Deposition No, 72.

"At Gniewkowo I saw a group of men who had barricaded themselves in a half-built house. There were four or five of them, armed with a machine-gun. They had to be tackled with hand-grenades.

"More than once I saw men who had been dropped by parachute. They were armed with light machine-guns and grenades. Close to Toruń seven were captured in my presence.

"Corporal St. W., who took part in suppressing the diversionist operations at Bydgoszcz, declares that the Germans had placed a machine-gun on the roof of the Protestant church in Danzig Street, and that all along this street there was firing from windows at passing Polish military forces, and at the civilian population also.

"During the suppression of the diversionists almost two hundred persons were captured with arms, and were shot. The bodies were laid out on the square. In all probability the Germans found them still unburied when they entered Bydgoszcz.

"I saw a number of aeroplanes shot down. In many cases they were piloted by young men who had studied in our schools, Polish citizens who had fled to Germany. They all had the rank of officer. The majority of them were drunk, and frequently they were allowed to take their 'fiancées' with them, making a particular display of cruelty at such times.

"Siedlce was badly devastated, but it was the town of Illow, near Gostynin, which made the most terrible impression upon me. The Staff of our retreating army was to have made its headquarters there. At the last moment the Staff halted in the village of Laski, quite close to Illow. The Germans began to bomb the little town an hour later. The bombing went on for twelve hours, from 6 a.m. to 6 p.m. When we passed through Illow later it was nothing more than a heap of smoking ruins. This fact sufficiently indicates the information service provided by the local Germans."

By a Lieutenant Colonel attached to the Polish Army General Staff:[104]
"In the area of operations of the army in Pomorze it was discovered that between September 8th and 10th three Germans disguised as Polish officers were driving around in a Buick car bearing the registration number

---

[104] Lieutenant Colonel K., attached to the Army General Staff, Deposition No. 109.

64028. The men spoke to soldiers, gave them tobacco of Danzig origin, and tried to persuade them to desert.

"In Pomorze, subversive agents armed with rifles and light machine-guns fired on trains, destroyed telephone cables, etc.

"Some definite instances:

"At Bydgoszcz on September 2nd/3rd.

"At Solec Kujawski, September 5th and 7th. The agents took possession of the local Protestant church, and from its tower machine-gunned the road from Bydgoszcz to Toruń.

"At Inowroclaw, September 7th (firing from windows at the 16th Infantry Division as it passed through the town)."

From a Polish Major:[105]

"German agents in Polish soldiers' uniforms mingled with Polish regiments, passing themselves off as belonging to regiments broken up by the enemy. They spread demoralization among our soldiers, and informed the enemy of their movements.

"The I56th Infantry Regiment, which was in the Niepołomice Forest, was attacked at night by Germans who had been led there by agents. In the course of the fight a group of German agents disguised as Polish soldiers opened fire on the true Polish soldiers. One of the agents shot the commander, Kubasiewicz, at point-blank range, as he stood surrounded by his men. The agent was killed at once; all he had on him was German money; he had no documents."

From a Polish engineer:[106]

"Owing to the fact that the agents were equipped with wireless transmitting and receiving sets, rocket-pistols, electric lamps, etc., they were able to place themselves quickly in contact with the German air force and motorized units, and a very dense network of espionage was organized. Captain M. noted a case of espionage in which the agents were a man in Polish officer's uniform, and a woman.

"On September 6th, 1939, the 8th Infantry Regiment left its barracks, which had been bombed by German aeroplanes, and fell back

---

[105] Major R., Deposition No. 118.
[106] Engineer Ch. B., Deposition No. 91.

upon a neighbouring place named Slawinek. The German aeroplanes appeared again, but did not bomb the barracks this time, but only the place at which the Regiment had arrived."

From a commander in the Polish Infantry:[107]
"On September 19th, 1939, close to Rzęsna Ruska, a spy wearing Polish uniform signalled objectives to the enemy artillery by means of rockets."

From a Polish officer attached to the Army General Staff:[108]
"The headquarters of the army at Lwów were situated in the building of a high school in Piekarska Street. The headquarters were bombed six hours after they had been transferred to this school. The same evening a beggar roaming in the neighbourhood of the place was arrested on suspicion. On him was found an exact list of objectives which had been bombed previously."

From a Polish Captain:[109]
"It was definite and proved several times over that from the outbreak of hostilities telephonic and telegraphic conversations were often intercepted. In the neighbourhood of Sniadow, for instance, a wire was found connected at one end to the telephone cable, while the other end was in a house on the route of the cable.

"The spot where the staff of our operative group was situated was regularly bombed, at the latest, twenty-four hours after we had taken up our quarters."

From a Polish officer of the Divisional General Staff:[110]
"The German armies had at their disposal a vast network of espionage in all the terrains in which operations went on. Our staff, which was established in a lonely house standing between a village and a forest in the neighbourhood of Piotrków, was surprised by enemy tanks on

---

[107] Lieutenant Colonel K., commanding an infantry regiment, Deposition No. 92.
[108] Lieutenant Colonel G., attached to Army General Staff, Deposition No. 93.
[109] Captain M., Deposition No. 94.
[110] Captain K., Divisional General Staff, Deposition No. 105.

September 5th, 1939. A short time before a crimson rocket had been seen shooting up above the forest."

From a Lieutenant of the Polish Sappers:[111]

"A Protestant pastor in the vicinity of Modlin regularly intercepted telephonic communications and destroyed the telephone cables. A domiciliary visit to his house led to the discovery of a wireless transmitter.

"In the neighbourhood of Modlin Germans living in the outskirts of this fortified place signalled the existence of an important army depot by setting fire to three houses close by. The depot was situated in the centre of the triangle thus marked out."

Organization of Fuel Depots in Poland

One proof of the vast ramifications of the German subversive activity and of the employment of the German minority to this end is the discovery in many parts of Poland of numerous fuel depots, established before the war and cleverly camouflaged.

From a Polish Lieutenant:[112]

"In a works for the manufacture of rubber articles, at Sanok, a secret store of petrol was found. It had been set up by a man named Otto Schmidt, who was director of the works. It was used by a German motorized division which reached Sanok. The German officer in command of the division possessed detailed plans which enabled him to find the store easily."

From an officer of the Polish Army General Staff:[113]

"From statements obtained, it is established that the German colonists concealed a certain quantity of petrol fuels."

---

[111] Lieutenant of Sappers, K., Deposition No. 106.
[112] Lieutenant S., Deposition No. 12.
[113] Lieutenant Colonel F., attached to Army General Staff, Deposition No. 13.

98

From another officer of the General Staff:[114]

"A battalion of motorized German infantry advanced in the direction of Lwów on September 13th or 14th. It was convoyed by several tanks, which halted in the vicinity of Kleparow. It was repulsed by a Polish counter-attack, and we captured a patrol led by a guide in civilian dress. The commander of this patrol stated that he had been searching for a store of petrol which was to be found in the neighbourhood of Kleparow. And, in fact, we discovered bidons of petrol buried in the ground close to the road."

From a Reserve Second Lieutenant:[115]

"On September 7th six German tanks halted on the highroad close to Wyszków. A German alighted from the leading tank and, after consulting a map, gave a signal with his horn. At this signal two men alighted and began to dig not far from a kilometre post and brought to light an iron barrel, which probably contained petrol."

---

[114] Lieutenant Colonel G., of Army General Staff, Deposition No. 54.
[115] Reserve Second Lieutenant S., Deposition No. 15.

CHAPTER FIVE - GERMAN JUSTICE

THE depositions quoted in preceding chapters sufficiently demonstrate the role played by the German minority in the German-Polish military campaign. German propaganda will endeavour to deny the authenticity of these dispositions. It must therefore be emphasised that all these accounts have been supplied by reliable eye-witnesses, though, for obvious reasons, their names cannot be disclosed until the end of the German occupation of Poland. They all establish the very important part played during the military operations by the German diversionist agents in Poland. Furthermore, their evidence is corroborated by the German Press itself, which has been by no means reluctant to discuss the diversionist agents' activities.

Thanks to the prolixity of that Press, the reader is bound to lose his last doubt as to the justice of the charge that the German minority in Poland betrayed the State of which it was a part. That Press will inform him that even during the war, contrary to the lies spread by the Germans, the Poles maintained an amazingly tolerant attitude towards the members of the German minority. This fact was admitted by the head of the Germans in Stanisławów, Dr. Zöckler, in the periodical, *Deutsche Arbeit*. When the war broke out he was arrested by the Polish police and held in the prison at Stanisławów. Zöckler admitted that he was treated well there, and his statement to this effect in the *Deutsche Arbeit* was quoted by the official organ of the German occupation authorities in Silesia, the *Kattowitzer Zeitung*, in its issue for February 14, 1940.
To convey adequately the role which the Third Reich assigned to the German minority in Poland, it is worthwhile quoting certain declarations made by particularly competent officials.

Here is what Dr. Goebbels himself said, when speaking, on December 2, 1939, to the local German population at Poznań:

"The indescribable sacrifices which were made by all in this province at the beginning of the war, in order to bring the precious German Folk back to the Reich, testify to the heroism of which our people are capable in this war."[116]

Speaking in Cracow, December 21, 1939, Dr. Frank[117] also declared that the alleged sacrifices made by the Germans in Poland were not made in vain, because they had been compensated for by the achievement of liberty.

The incredible cynicism of this statement is obvious when it is recalled that the lands to which this "liberty" has been brought are areas which have been Polish for a thousand years, areas in which the Polish population has always been over 90 percent of the total, while the Germans, even according to German sources, constituted only 5 to 6 percent. In the town of Bydgoszcz Poles were 91 percent of the total population, in Poznań they were 97 per cent, in Toruń 96 percent, in Gdynia 99 percent. The rural areas also were purely Polish.

The Germans do not spare public pronouncements which confirm the fact of the German minority's hostile activities against the Polish State. The following remarks concerning the Germans of Cieszyn Silesia, published in the *Dresdener Neueste Nachrichten* for November 2, 1939, are decidedly revealing:

"Behind the Viennese sentiment there are skulls as hard as iron, stand men like those of Egerland or Bohmerwald. They have not made any national compromise, they are not to be turned aside on this point. They were already having to fight for their German nationality at a time when the Germans in Eastern Upper Silesia still seemed completely secure in the great German Kaiser Reich. It is no accident that the Führer of the Silesian Germans in Poland, Wiesner, comes from Bielitz."[118]

The "Führers" of the German minority in Poland threw off their mask immediately after Germany had occupied Poland.

---

[116] *"Die unsagbaren Opfer die in dieser Provinz von allen bei Beginn des Krieges gebracht worden sind um wertvolles deutsches Volkstum ins Reich zuruckführen, bezeugen welchen Heldentums unser Volk in diesem Kriege fähig ist." (Völkischer Beobachter.* December 3, 1939.)

[117] Governor-General of that part of German-occupied Poland not "incorporated" into the Reich.

[118] *"Hinter dem Wiener Gefühl stecken eisenharte Schädel, stehen Männer wie die Egerländer oder Böhmerwäldler. Sie haben nie ein nationales Kompromiss geschlossen, sie sind in diesen Punkt nie zurückzuweisen. Sie haben schon kämpfen müssen für ihr Deutschtum damals, als der Deutsche in Ostoberschlesien noch fest geborgen schien in grossen Deutschen Kaiserreich. Es ist kein Zufall, dass der Führer des schlesischen Deutschtums in Polen, Wiesner, aus Bielitz stammt." (Article entitled: "Deutsche Städte im neuen Reichsgebiet.")*

The former member of the Polish Senate, M. Wiesner, the 'loyal' leader of the German minority, is going the rounds in Germany, spitting out the worst of insults against Poland, and representing the Polish State as a centre of perpetual 'terror.'[119] These leaders always participate in the days of liberation triumphantly organized in all the territories incorporated into the Reich.

"A fanfare," says the description of one such celebration at Katowice, *"heralded the beginning of the announcement of freedom. To the strains of the military march and the jubilation of the people the Gauleiter and Governor of Silesia, Joseph Wagner, inspected all the membership. He was accompanied by Lieutenant-General Brandt, Major-General von Knobelsdorf, the Deputy Gauleiter Bracht, the head of the civil administration Fitzner, and the two leaders of the German group in Eastern Upper Silesia, Rudolf Wiesner (Bielitz), the leader of the Jungdeutsche Partei for Poland, and Dr. Ulitz (Katowice), the leader of the German Volksbund for Upper Silesia. Afterward the Gauleiter and those accompanying him took up their positions on the platform, and the Gauorganisationsleiter reported that 22 standards and banners and over 30,000 German comrades from all over Upper Silesia were present."*[120]

The activity of all the varieties of German minority leaders is revealed not only in the various types of organization. It is clear from innumerable depositions which give the exact names that these allegedly loyal leaders of the German minority have displayed incredible bestiality in regard to the Poles since the German troops occupied the Polish territory. For what else could such individuals as Heinze Brandt and Gerhard Joschke (the latter being the brother of the *Kreisleiter* of

---

[119] *Kattowitzer Zeitung*, February 2, 1940.

[120] *"Ein Fanfarensignal kundete den Beginn der Freiheitskundgebung an. Unter der Klängen des Präsentiermarsches und unter dem Jubel der Bevölkerung schritt der Gauleiter und Oberpräsident von Schlesien Joseph Wagner die Ehrenbereitschaften aller Gliederungen ab. In seiner Begleitung befand sich Generalleutnant Brandt, Generalmajor von Knobelsdorf, der Stellvertretende Gauleiter Bracht, der Chef der Zivilverwaltung Fitzner und die beiden Führer der Deutschen Volksgruppen in Ostoberschlesien, Rudolf Wiesner (Bielitz), der Landesleiter der Jungdeutschen Partei für Polen und Dr. Ulitz (Kattowitz) der Leiter des Deutschen Volksbundes für Oberschlesien. Danach nahm der Gauleiter mit seiner Begleitung auf der Ehrentribune Aufstellung, während ihnen der Gauorganisationsleiter meldete dass hier 22 Standarten und Fahnen und über 30,000 deutsche Volksgenossen aus dem ganzen Oberschlesischen Raum angetreten seien."* (Breslauer Neueste Nachrichten, October 16, 1939.)

Katowice) occupy themselves with, if not denouncing Poles? Both these men are Polish citizens parading about the streets of Katowice in uniform. How many human lives are on the consciences of these traitors to the Polish State, these traitors who, the day after the German occupation of Silesia, resumed the uniforms of the German field army? Here is a deposition made on January 29, 1940, by a Pole of Katowice, living at Orzegow:

"I observed in my village that the former group of contrabandists collaborated actively with the Germans. Also several former officials in the local administration and in the briquette works. Thus Strączek, Gornik, Klinzer, and Krauze have been kept in their jobs by the Germans because they were members of the Volksbund."

The same Pole goes on to say that it afterwards transpired that numerous police officials collaborated with the Germans. One police official who was out of work and without means of subsistence offered his services to the Germans. They answered that he could not be admitted as he had not formerly worked in a German organization.

All these police officials, Germans who had passed themselves off as Poles, assisted the occupation authorities in the work of "cleansing" the territory of undesirable elements by denouncing Poles living in the area. The hero of a notorious trial in pre-war days, the manufacturer, Beckmann, who was charged with injury to the Polish nation, now enjoys great regard among the Germans at Cracow. Beckmann has permission to visit the Montelupi prison from time to time, and on these visits he tortures the public prosecutor detained there who was responsible for charging him.

Here is another deposition which indicates the part played by the German minority after the occupation of Poznań, and especially in the town of Leszno:

"At Leszno, those specially engaged in the extermination of the Polish population include first and foremost the detachment of the Gestapo with its head, the Polizeirat Grunt, then the Burgomaster of Baumbach, Dr. Schneider, Pastor Wolfgang Bickerich, Baron Losen of Drzeczkow, the wife

of the head of the German high school (I do not remember the name), Leon Zabka, a butcher (he was responsible for the death of the schoolboy Hanca). In addition, with a few rare exceptions, all the German population in the district collaborated with the occupation authorities. A large number of them ostentatiously demanded further executions."

Among the Germans who were particularly enraged against the Poles here were Malcherek, Pine, and Duda.

Another deposition mentions the names of Germans who were outstanding in this regard at Kościan.

"Among the Germans of particular 'merit' must be mentioned the Gestapo detachment, the magistrate Lize, Burgomaster Schreiter, the former Burgomaster Heinze, who was afterwards appointed school inspector, the landowner Lorenty, the official Ischdonat.

"The German population of the district took an active part in all the persecutions. One person who particularly distinguished herself was Frau von Hofmannswaldau of Koszanowo, near Smigiel, who was continually importuning the Gestapo and the magistrate, with demands to proceed to further executions."

Such examples could be added to without end. They testify to the fact that the German minority in Poland did not cease its treacherous activities when the German troops occupied Poland. Besides openly organizing themselves into the structure of the Third Reich, they proceeded to help in the extermination of the Polish population, exposing them to terrible atrocities and to the bestialities of the Gestapo.

This procedure is still going on. Though many months have passed since Germany's treacherous aggression against Poland, aided by the treachery of the German minority within Poland, not a day passes undisturbed by the groans of Poles martyred and condemned to terrible suffering by the Reich's spies and informers, citizens of the Polish State.

Since the German occupation of Poland the Reich authorities have been brutally deporting the Polish elements from their age-old homes in the "incorporated" Polish areas. At night the Gestapo agents drive thousands of Polish families from their houses and dwellings, allowing them to take only a small suitcase and fifty marks per person. Everything else: land, house, dwellings and all the furniture, clothing, linen, ready money, and even family keepsakes, are pillaged without compensation. The evicted people are carried in cattle trucks to the "General Gouvernement," where they are turned out at a wayside station without food, without money, and with no roof over their heads. Frequently this journey lasted several days or more; during the hard winter of 1939-40 thousands of people, especially women and children, were frozen to death on such journeys.

Poles still left in the "incorporated" areas also have their lands, houses, factories, shops, workshops, etc., confiscated without compensation.

Throughout all occupied Poland there have been terrible massacres of innocent people, while tens of thousands of people are being tortured in prisons and concentration camps.

All Polish cultural life has been completely suppressed. The Polish universities and high schools have been closed; the Polish libraries, museums, art galleries and scientific laboratories have been stripped, and their more valuable possessions carried off to Germany. Polish national and religious monuments have been destroyed. In the "incorporated" areas all Polish inscriptions have been removed. Both Catholic and Protestant churches have to endure terrible persecution. Hundreds of clergy have been shot or tortured to death in prisons and concentration camps.

These monstrous crimes against the Polish nation, its civilization and culture, leave no room for doubt as to the purpose of the German allegations of Polish "maltreatment" of the German minority. It is obvious today that the Germans had long planned the systematic destruction of everything Polish, in order to wipe the very name of Poland from the earth. In order to justify such an iniquity to the world it was necessary to represent that the Polish nation was so barbarous, as demonstrated by its treatment of the German minority, that it deserved no less a fate. Thus, the lie about the alleged Polish atrocities (*polnische Greueltaten*) is intended to vindicate the terrible truth of the German occupation in Poland.

For Services Rendered...

It is not surprising that there should have been munificent rewards for the leaders who distinguished themselves in subversive activities and the practice of treachery and diversion. The *Essener National-Zeitung* for January 25, 1940, announced that the same Wiesner who, by the way, fled from Poland a little before the outbreak of hostilities, spoke at a meeting in Stuttgart on "the sufferings and the liberation of the Germans in Poland." The *Deutsches Auslands-Institut*, already referred to previously as one of the most important centres for espionage, awarded Wiesner a silver medal for his "labours."

But the crowning glory for these persons came when the six leaders of the German minority in Poland were decorated by Hitler himself with gold insignia of honour. The six leaders were photographed at the time and the *Völkischer Beobachter* for October 22, 1939, identified each by name.

Illustration of Germans Living in Poland Rewarded for Aiding the Wehrmacht during the Invasion

Aufn.: BDM.-Bildstelle

Der Führer verlieh Goldene Ehrenzeichen an sechs volksdeutsche Führer aus dem ehemaligen Polen

Von links nach rechts: Ludwig Wolff-Lodz, Dr. Ulitz-Kattowitz, Gauleiter Wagner-Breslau, Senator Wiesner-Bielitz, ff-Obergruppenführer Lorenz, Senator Hasbach-Hermannshof, Gero Freiherr von Gersdorff (in Vertretung von Dr. Kohnert-Bromberg) und Weiß-Jarotschin

LEADERS OF THE GERMAN MINORITY IN POLAND
DECORATED BY HITLER WITH GOLD MEDALS FOR
THEIR FIFTH COLUMN ACTIVITIES

A photograph published in the official Nazi organ
Völkischer Beobachter

"From left to right: Ludwig Wolff (Łódź), Dr. Ulitz (Kattowitz), Gauleiter Wagner (Breslau), Senator Wiesner (Bielitz), Obergruppenführer Lorenz, Senator Hasbach (Hermannshoff), Gero Freiherr von Gersdorff (representing Dr. Kohnert, Bromberg), and Weiss (Jarotchin)."

108

After the existing German organizations had been "incorporated," they were rapidly dissolved and automatically absorbed into the N.S.D.A.P. A meeting at Bydgoszcz on January 21, 1940, was devoted to the dissolution of the *Deutsche Vereinigung*, numbering 70,000 members and 260 sections. Taking the place of the president, Hans Kohnert, another minority leader, the S.S. Sturmbannführer, Dr. Gero von Gersdorff, made a speech. The *Völkischer Beobachter* for January 21, 1940, describes the occasion in the following words:

"The final demonstration of the members of the Deutsche Vereinigung was a demonstration of their fidelity to Adolf Hitler, to the Reich, and to the Fatherland, of which they have given proof over twenty years, facing death, the Polish terror of that valorous fidelity which in the future also they put at the Führer's disposition."

A large number of German newspapers (among others the *Frankfurter Zeitung* for January 30, 1940) published a report of a meeting of National-Socialist Party leaders at which Herr Greiser presided. The meeting was devoted to consideration of problems arising out of organizing the German minority. They discussed the *Volksdienst* (compulsory agricultural instruction for the youth), the *Landjahrlager* (the twelve-month rural camps for youth leaving school), the *Gauschulungsburg* (places for instruction in Nazi philosophy), the *Gaugrenzamt* (a department devoted to research on German minority questions), and other forms of organization in which the Germans of the *Warthegau*, i.e. the illegally annexed Western Poland, were to be systematically grouped, after the former minority organizations had been dissolved. It was stated, *inter alia*, that the *Hitler-Jugend* based its activities on the former organizations of German youth. The report declared that the organization of the party was already complete, so far as the higher authorities were concerned. Those who previously had been the leaders of the German minority were now represented in the *Gau*. Thirty-two out of a total of forty-two districts (including the province of Łódź) were provided with leaders, and among these the heads of the minority *Jungdeutsche Partei* and the *Deutscher Volksbund* had been appointed for the town of Łódź and the district of Łódź. Herr Greiser stated that he had had great difficulties with appointments to minor party posts, as he had only Germans of Poznańia (in other words, members of the German minority) at his disposition, and though these were very strong in regard to their convictions, they had only a poor acquaintance with political problems.

This long report calls for no comment. Only a few months after the "incorporation" all the German minority is being rapidly absorbed into the ranks of the Hitler organization as a compact and organized group, united in the one thought and the one sentiment.

In the report quoted an organization referred to by the name of *Selbstschutz* was mentioned. Under the Polish regime this consisted of formations of Nazi secret fighting units, which, after the "incorporation," were transformed into an auxiliary paramilitary organization, composed solely of members of the former German minority intended for fighting the Poles. It appears from the report that the *Selbstschutz* will soon form sections of the S.A. and S.S.

In the *Völkischer Beobachter* for February 18, 1940, is a description of the nature of the *Selbstschutz*. It is a kind of auxiliary police composed of German minority elements from Poland. The party organ, with perfect cynicism, remarks of this auxiliary police composed of "loyal" Germans that their knowledge of Polish will enable them to discover the most secret refuges of the Poles, and in any case they have been the most reliable of informers. The police owes them a great deal. In other words, the German minority has directly contributed to the application of terrorism against the Poles.

The organ of the German occupation authorities, the *Ostdeutscher Beobachter*, also gives some characteristic details of the task which has been entrusted to the *Volksdeutsche* elements organized in special formations of the *Selbstschutz*. The newspaper recognizes that in the occupied territory the members of the German minority in Poland are the right hand of the police in the repressive measures applied to the Polish population.

The task of these secret agents of the Gestapo has been facilitated, says the *Ostdeutscher Beobachter*, by their profound knowledge of Poland and the Polish language.

In its issue for February 4, 1940, the *Kattowitzer Zeitung* announced that in the provinces of Silesia three battalions intended to act as auxiliary police, consisting of one thousand men aged between eighteen and thirty-five and recruited from among the German minority in Silesia, have recently been formed. The official organ of the occupation authorities ends its report on these police with the joyous realization that "soon now there will be police drawn from the local population in the streets of Silesia."

But that is not all. The Germans of Poland who gratefully endorse the doctrine of Hitlerism are at present taking all kinds of educational courses and training. In its issue for February 15, 1940, the *Völkischer Beobachter* refers to one such course. It was an S.A. course. Their chief, Lutze, himself spoke to the loyal Germans of Poland. Among those present must be mentioned the head of the *Warthe* group, Group Leader Ivers, and the head of the *Vistula group*, Brigade Leader Hacker.

Under the rod of the central authorities the German Press reports all these things without the least embarrassment, and, on the contrary, quite openly. With complete cynicism the *Schlesische Zeitung* declares that a large number of Germans, resident in Poland, and Polish citizens, gave incalculable aid to the German army during the war, through their service of espionage and advance posts. The same fact is frankly admitted in the propaganda publication *Unsere Flieger über Polen*,[121] issued in Berlin, which gives the story told by four officers. In it is a narrative called "*Männer und Taten*."[122] In the introduction to this narrative we read:

"That is why I want to tell you about the death of non-commissioned officer Steinbeiss and the heroic rescue of three soldiers achieved by a German peasant. At nightfall I saw a boat with two men in it coming down the river. I called to them in German, and they answered in German. They came nearer, and I saw that they were Polish soldiers. They had their weapons with them, and I was very frightened.

---

[121] *Our Airmen over Poland.*
[122] *The Men and the Deeds.*

"Perkun came and reported: 'The group is ready for action, Herr Major.' I had to go to my car. Reingraber happened to go by, and above the noise of the engine he shouted to me: 'They were deserters, Herr Major, two deserters who want to come over to the Germans, and I have brought them along with me as prisoners.'"[123]

The episode reported occurred in Pomorze, early in the war. German airmen were aided by two Germans of Polish citizenship, Stricke from Weitzenau, and Wruck. Every day Wruck brought the soldiers food and also precise information concerning the movements of the Polish troops. Warned by Wruck, the German airmen left their hiding-place, and "in the hills south of Jabłonowo came upon the German advanced posts, exactly as Wruck had said they would."

From articles, photographs, and descriptions given in the German Press only one conclusion can be drawn: the German element in Poland was an outpost organized by conquering Hitlerism. During the first few months of the German occupation this element was automatically integrated with the Nazi organization into which it was dissolved. The "minority organizations" all served only as camouflage for irredentist activity. That activity was carried on before and during the war on orders from Berlin, and the minority constituted an innumerable army of spies and diversionist agents which worked to weaken the Polish armed forces and to destroy the Polish State.

---

[123] *"Als es beinahe Nacht war, ich sah ein Boot mit zwei Männern die den Fluss herunterruderten. Ich rief sie deutsch an, und sie antworteten deutsch. Sie kamen heran, and ich sah, dass as Polnische Soldaten waren. Sie hatten ihre Waffen bei sich, und ich war sehr erschrocken...*

"Perkun kommt and meldet: 'Gruppe stattbereit, Herr Major.' Ich muss zu meinen Maschine. Reingraber laüft neben mir her und noch durch das Brüllen der Motoren schreit er mir zu: 'Es waren Deserteure, Herr Major, beide Deserteure, die überlaufen wollen zu den Deutschen, and ich habe sie als Gefangene mitgebracht.'" (Op. cit., p. 143)

CHAPTER SIX - SOME GENERAL CONCLUSIONS

POLAND was not the only country in which the German minority was called to fulfil a strictly defined task of espionage and diversionist activity. The same task was incumbent upon all the German minorities which in German literature are denominated *Grenzminderheiten* (frontier minorities). There were said to be some fifteen to twenty millions of them, scattered throughout all the States of Europe, not excluding the Germans in Italy, in the Scandinavian countries, above all in Denmark, and also the Germans resident in France, in other words, in a country which the Germans hated as much as they hated Poland, and which in Mein Kampf Hitler regarded as a foremost enemy of the Reich.

After the 1914-18 war these minorities were assigned the role of levers, with the aid of which the problem of a New European Order was to be resolved.

In addition to the minority Germans, other national minorities, living in the areas of the respective States, were to play an auxiliary role in the disintegration of internal order. Both the Governments of the Weimar Republic and that of the Third Reich organized intrigues and corruption, and lavishly subsidized all subversive and centrifugal movements in neighbouring countries.

After Hitler came to power, yet another ally was utilized. This was the local political groups who accepted the National-Socialist or Fascist ideology, and who were so blinded that they were ready to endanger the independence of their countries in order to carry through their own internal political games. In their ranks were also a large number of common traitors and German spies.[124]

These groups, on the lines of the Quisling organization in Norway, were undoubtedly of great service to Hitler's operations even though they represented only a small, and mainly quite insignificant, section of their national communities.

In September, 1939, the Germans in Poland constituted an army of conspirators and spies which was only awaiting the order from Berlin.

---

[124] This does not apply to Poland, where no such allies were to be found.

Obeying orders, during the September campaign this army developed especially extensive activity. But Poland was not the only field in which it has operated.

The events which have followed in the course of military operations have in fact revealed that this army of conspirators and spies was spread in all the other countries of Europe. It has been demonstrated that the German diversionist agents took possession of Denmark, that in Norway those agents were everywhere, and that the famous attack made by the German airmen on Nyversum was organized with their aid. By means of wireless transmitters they furnished the German staff with information just as they did in Poland, informing them of the precise situation of King Haakon, the Norwegian authorities, and the diplomatic corps.

A similar network of spies, saboteurs, and diversionists of all kinds was scattered over France and Belgium. The internal disintegration of these countries and the establishment of the espionage and diversionist network was carried out by various, very subtle methods; one of the most important was the assiduous cultivation of "the German minority" in Alsace and Lorraine, and in the districts of Eupen and Malmedy.

In the review *Suddeutsche Monatshefte*, M. Hassenblatt, the legal adviser to all the German minorities, wrote in 1929:

"One has only to glance at the agitation which exists in Alsace or at the situation of the Germans in Belgium, Eupen, and Malmedy, as well as in the north, in German Schleswig, to be convinced that a number of problems of a juridical nature remain still to be solved in Europe. These problems must be solved not only in the east of Europe, where the mingling of the nations is most apparent, but also on other frontiers where strong agglomerations of Germans are settled"

In 1928 an article appeared in the review *Elsass Lothringens Heimatstimmen*, published in Berlin, which sought to dispose of "the legend of French unity." It is characteristic that articles of this kind were always accompanied by organized action. Such action was pursued even in the period of Franco-German "collaboration" during the Stresemann-Briand conversations. The action was inspired by the opinion which Hitler-Germany expressed about France: "France is condemned to

114

death." That was the slogan of the German Press at the beginning of 1940.

Apart from the plots in Alsace and Lorraine, attempts were made to create artificial "nationalities" within the frontiers of France, such as the "Breton nation." The results of all these intrigues, on which tens and hundreds of millions of marks were expended quickly became evident; from the very beginning of the 1939-40 war the French courts were occupied with the espionage and diversionist activities of various Alsace-Lorraine "autonomists," and even Breton "nationalists." The leader of these "nationalists" proved to be a common German spy. He fled to Germany, and the French court sentenced him to death in his absence.

The extent to which all this activity conduced to France's military breakdown in May and June is difficult at present to determine. In any case, the stories told by British and Poles who were in France at the time of the German Army's break through, and who only later made their way to Great Britain, contain certain extremely characteristic details. For instance, in various localities of central France, where the population evacuated from Alsace and Lorraine were accommodated, there was no lack of ostensibly loyal French citizens, who welcomed the Nazist troops as they entered the streets by giving the Nazi salute and shouting "*Heil Hitler.*" These stories definitely confirmed that they were people who formerly had always stressed their fidelity to France and hostility to Germany.

How many of them were spies who had engaged in sending important military and political information to the German authorities by means of wireless transmitters? In any case the "traitor from Stuttgart," Ferdonnet, boasted in one of his broadcasts that there were two hundred short-wave wireless transmitters on French soil, supplying information to the German intelligence service.

Some days before the invasion of Holland and Belgium an article written by the military correspondent of the *Tribune de Lausanne* appeared in that newspaper. The article suggested methods of fighting German diversionist activity in the event of an invasion of Switzerland, and was inspired by the experiences of the countries which had been victims of aggression, and also by a consciousness of the danger of diversionist activities which threatened the Swiss.

On April 21 last, which is Hitler's birthday, an appeal entitled *Deutscher Junge, Deutsches Mädel* (German Boy, German Girl) was distributed throughout Switzerland. The appeal invited the German youth to swell the ranks of the organization known as *Reichsdeutsche Jugend im Auslande*. It contained the following sentence:

"A passive belief alone is of no benefit to Germany. The German youth living abroad must therefore flock together into a community that does not live a doubly fruitful life for the benefit of others, but only as our homeland strives towards a greater future."[125]

The impudence of such a procedure inspired the author of the article in the *Tribune de Lausanne* to make deductions of a practical nature which, as the Polish experience showed, must be applied by the civilian population in the event of a German invasion:

"Suspects must be arrested before they have time to do any destruction; the authors of sabotage, the spreaders of false news must be overcome by force. For all the national territory there is only one order of the day: wherever the enemy is met he will be killed. If this enemy rises everywhere at once, it will be necessary to organize detachments in each village, charged with attacking the troops brought by air or donning uniforms when the conflict begins.

"There is no lack of men capable of fulfilling these tasks. Let our old riflemen, our old sportsmen take out their carbines, their old-fashioned rifles, their sporting guns, let them put on their former uniforms or simple brassards. They will show that it is not necessary to weaken the effective strength of the army in order to guarantee the security of the rear.

"There is not a country in the world which is better prepared to put up opposition to the new methods of warfare. Our diligent shooting practice, our cantonal and federal fetes will have served not only to

---

[125] *"Ein stiller Glaube allein, wird für Deutschland keinen Nutzen zeitigen können. Die Auslandsdeutsche Jugend muss sich deshalb zusammenscharen zu einer Gemeinschaft, die nicht zur Freude anderer ein zwietrachtiges Leben führt, sondern wie unsere Heimat einer grossen Zeit entgegenstrebt."*

provide us with excellent fighters, but also to maintain the over-ages in form. The hour is come to organize all the forces available. The father will fight by his own house; the son will do his duty at the front.”[126]

In this connection we may be permitted to refer to a report which reveals the methods which Switzerland had to adopt against its internal enemies. The following is the text of a message from *The Times* correspondent at Geneva, sent on November 20, 1940:

“The Swiss Federal Government has dissolved the so-called Swiss National Movement, a totalitarian organization closely connected with some Nazi bodies, and some of the leaders of which went as official delegates to the Nuremberg congress.

“Inquiries recently made show that the movement aims at transforming Swiss institutions not by constitutional methods, but by illegal means and contrary to Swiss tradition. These means include secret instructions to members to form cells and groups and semi-military fighting units among youth. Such a movement is regarded as being likely seriously to endanger public order and to create uneasiness and even conflict among the population.

“The Swiss National Movement last week approached the Federal Government and claimed that the former adherents of the Frontist Movement, the predecessor of the Swiss National Movement, who were prosecuted and sentenced, be rehabilitated and allowed again to hold meetings and publish their newspapers. The claim was rejected by the Federal Government, who will not allow any intrigues or mischief-making in home affairs.”[127]

The “Fifth Column” also attempted and is still attempting to operate in Great Britain, but here its activities came up against the solid resistance and watchful opinion of the British public, and the effective counteraction of the British police and counterespionage service. Unable to resort to internal diversionist activities of a military nature, the agents of the Third Reich have endeavoured—quite in vain it has to be said—to

---

[126] Quoted from *Le Temps*. May 8, 1940.
[127] *The Times*, November 21, 1940.

spread a defeatist spirit among the people of Great Britain and to undermine confidence in the British Government. Their efforts in this direction are equally surely doomed to failure.

The Third Reich has found more suitable material for diversionist work in the United States, if only owing to the heterogeneous composition of the great North American Republic in racial and national regards. Within the frontiers of the United States live, among others, over ten million persons of German origin, and a certain number of these are consciously ardent Germans.

The experiences of the 1914-1918 world war were of themselves sufficient to make the United States pay close attention to German diversionist activities on their territory. But the recent investigations into the plotting of the Hitlerite American Germans proved that, by the dimensions and the perfidy of its activities, the Third Reich has left the Germany of Wilhelm II far behind. The recent acts of sabotage in the American armament works and arsenals have again been an alarm signal for American public opinion.

One thing can be stated, namely, that in all the diversionist operations carried out in various countries Germany has never advanced beyond the methods which were applied in Poland and which were revealed in such a brilliant light during the September, 1939, campaign. For this reason the Polish experiences retain all their great value today for all the world.

APPENDIX ONE – CONFIDENTIAL ORDER ISSUED BY THE WEHRMACHT

THIS confidential Wehrmacht order was found on two German airmen September 2, 1939. A full translation follows the illustrations.

Illustrations of Confidential Wehrmacht Order

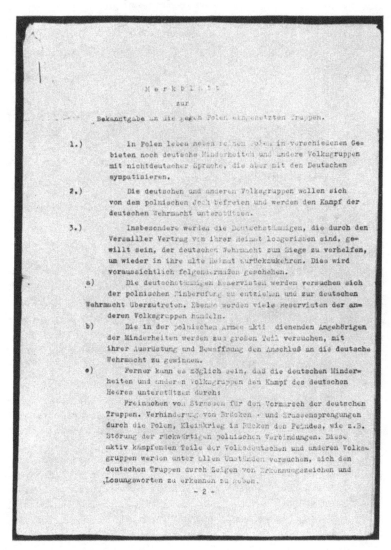

A CONFIDENTIAL ORDER ISSUED BY THE *WEHRMACHT*
This document was found on two German airmen brought down by
the Polish anti-aircraft defences near Poznán on September 2, 1939.

4.)   Diese Erkennungsmarken sind:

a)   rotes Tuch mit großem gelben Punkt in der Mitte, teil =
weiss in Taschentuchgrösse,

b)   hellblaue Armbinde mit gelbem Punkt in der Mitte,

c)   hellbraun - grauer Kombinationsanzug mit gelber Granate
auf Kragenspiegel und auf linkem Ärmel,

d)   es werden noch weitere Kräfte deutscher Minderheiten und
anderer Volksgruppen den Kampf des deutschen Heeres unter=
stützen. Sie tragen folgende Erkennungszeichen:
    1) Hakenkreuzarmbinden;
    2) Als Waffen Pistolen Nr. 14 u. 34 sowie gegebenenfalls
       Handgranaten tschechischen Musters,

e)   als Stichwort für Sämtliche: (deutsch, polnisch, ukrainisch
russisch und tschechisch)
                 " E c h o "
(überall gleich ausgesprochen wie geschrieben)

5)   Demgemäß ist das Verhalten des Gegners daraufhin zu be =
obachten, ob die verabredeten Erkennungszeichen auftreten
oder sonstige Anzeichen darauf hinweisen, daß bei dem gegen=
überliegenden Gegner Angehörige der Minderheiten zur Aufgabe
des Kampfes gewillt sind.

6.)   Es muß damit gerechnet werden, daß sich nicht alle Deutsch=
stämmigen und Angehörige anderer Volksgruppen der Wehrpflicht
entziehen können. Einzelne Angehörige dieser Gruppen werden
sicher aus besonderen Gründen in der polnischen Armee blei =
ben.

7.) a)   Die Angehörigen der Minderheiten, die sich der Wehrpflicht
entziehen oder im Kampf gefangen genommen werden, sind nach
Möglichkeit sofort von Soldaten rein polnischer Nationalität
zu trennen und zunächst wie Kriegsgefangene zu behandeln.
    Angehörige der Minderheiten, die zwar nicht für die Wehr=

- 3 -

Wehrmacht kampfmäßig eingesetzt sind, aber mit uns sympati =
sieren, können auch in regulärer polnischer Uniform und Be=
waffnung (Militär, Grenzschutz oder andere polnische Orga =
nisationsbekleidung) auftreten. Dabei wird es sich vor allem
um Überläufer oder solche Personen handeln, die in polnische
Kampfverband die Waffen strecken.

Diese Personen sind vorläufig als Kriegsgefangene zu be =
handeln, aber in den Gef.-Sammelstellen und Lagern von Ge =
fangenen rein polnischer Nationalität getrennt unterzubrin=
gen.

Das Gleiche gilt von anderen Angehörigen der Minderheiten,
die sich selbst der Truppe stellen oder ihr, z.B. durch die
geh. Feldpolizei zugeführt werden, sofern zu erwarten ist,
daß ihre eingehende Vernehmung in den Gef.-Lagern wertvolle
Ergebnisse haben könnte.

Soweit die Minderheiten - Angehörigen Waffen bei sich
führen, sind diese durch die Truppe zu sammeln und auf dem
Nachschubwege den Mun.-Lagern und Parks zuzuführen.

b)   Angehörige von Minderheiten, die für die Wehrmacht käm =
pfen bzw. von der Wehrmacht angesetzt sind, können auftreten:

    1) In regulärer polnischer Uniform und Ausrüstung. Sie
        werden aus den polnischen Kampfverbänden geschlossen
        oder einzeln überlaufen und sich zu erkennen geben.

    2) Als Civilisten.
        Kennzeichen: Vergl. Ziffer 4 d. Merkbl.

    3) Als Fallschirmabspringer mit grünlich - graubraunem
        Kombinationsanzug mit gelber Granate, eventuell auch
        in Civil. Sie sind bewaffnet und mit Sprengmittel aus=
        gerüstet.

Angehörige von Minderheiten, die für uns kämpfen,(vergl.
Ziffer 4) sind gesondert zu behandeln und dem zuständigen
Ic/A.O. des Grz.Sch.Abschn.Kdos.13 zuzuführen. Die Waffen
und anderen Kampfmittel dieser Leute sind gesondert zu
sammeln.

8.)   Es muß damit gerechnet werden, daß die Polen, deren Cha =
rakter sich durch Grausamkeit und Verschlagenheit auszeichnet
die deutschen Truppen täuschen werden durch Anwendung von
Maßnahmen, die auch die Deutschstämmigen anwenden.

9.)   Alle Wehrmachtangehörigen sind zu belehren, daß sie an
zahlreichen Stellen rein deutsches Gebiet mit überwiegend

- 4 -

deutscher Bevölkerung betreten. Ihr Auftreten muß dementspre...
Von der Haltung jedes Einzelnen wird es abhängen, ob die
Deutschstämmige Bevölkerung die Rückgliederung aller deutsch...
Landstriche an das Großdeutsche Reich freudig begrüßt.

Für die Richtigkeit:

[signature]

M a j o r .

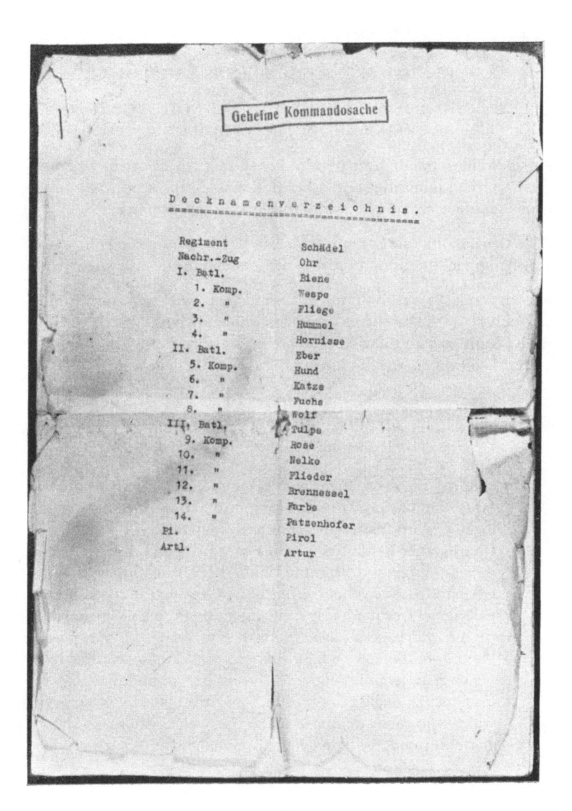

Docknamenverzeichnis.
=====================================

Regiment	Schädel
Nachr.-Zug	Ohr
I. Batl.	Biene
1. Komp.	Wespe
2. "	Fliege
3. "	Hummel
4. "	Hornisse
II. Batl.	Eber
5. Komp.	Hund
6. "	Katze
7. "	Fuchs
8. "	Wolf
III. Batl.	Tulpe
9. Komp.	Rose
10. "	Nelke
11. "	Flieder
12. "	Brennessel
13. "	Farbe
14. "	Patzenhofer
Pi.	Pirol
Artl.	Artur

Translation of the document follows:

CONFIDENTIAL ORDER ISSUED BY THE WEHRMACHT

INSTRUCTIONS TO BE BROUGHT TO THE NOTICE OF TROOPS
ENGAGED AGAINST POLAND

1.) In addition to inhabitants of pure Polish race, there are in various regions German minorities and other national groups speaking non-German languages, but who sympathize with the Germans.

2.) The German and other groups wish to be freed from the Polish yoke and will support the German Army (*Wehrmacht*) in the struggle.

3.) In particular, the inhabitants of German race who were torn from their country by the Treaty of Versailles will be disposed to aid the German Army to gain the victory in order to return to their former country. This will be accomplished probably in the following manner:

   a) The reservists of German race will attempt to avoid being mobilized in the Polish Army and to join the German Army. Many reservists belonging to other national groups will act similarly.
   b) Minority representatives who belong to active units of the Polish Army will to a large extent attempt to join the German Army, together with their equipment and weapons.
   c) On the other hand it is possible that the German minorities and those belonging to other national groups will support the German troops in their struggle: By clearing the roads for the passage of German troops; by preventing the Poles from blowing up the bridges and paved highways; by starting a minor war in the rear of the Poles as, for instance, by causing trouble to the Polish rear communications. These German nationals or elements belonging to other national groups actively struggling will in any case attempt to make themselves known to the German troops by employing special signs and passwords.

4.) These signs for making themselves known are:

a) A piece of red material usually the size of a handkerchief, with a large yellow spot in the centre.
b) Light blue brassards with a yellow spot in the centre.
c) A light grey-brown overall with a yellow grenade on the collar button and on the left sleeves.
d) Other forces forming part of the German minorities and other national groups will support the German Army in the struggle. They will carry the following distinctive marks:
    1) Brassards with swastikas.
    2) For weapons, pistols of type Nos. 14 and 34, and also, in certain cases, hand-grenades of Czech pattern.
e) The password for all participants (German, Polish, Ukrainian, Russian, and Czech):

"ECHO"

(as this word is everywhere written and pronounced in the same way).

5.) In conformity with the foregoing, it will be necessary to observe the opponent's attitude, in order to determine whether he is about to make the signs in question, or for other indications that we are confronted with minority representatives inclined to abandon the fight.

6.) In all cases it must be borne in mind that not all the men of German race and not all those belonging to other national groups will be able to evade military obligations. Certain members of these groups will definitely remain in the Polish Army for special reasons.

7.)

a) Members of minority races who have deserted or have been taken prisoner during the struggle will be separated at once and as much as possible from soldiers of purely Polish nationality and treated at first as prisoners of war. Members of minority races who are not engaged on the side of the *Wehrmacht*, but actively sympathize with us, may present themselves in Polish uniform and with the regular Polish weapons (dressed as military, frontier guards, or members of other Polish organizations). This will apply mainly to deserters or to individuals who lay down their arms in the Polish fighting forces. These individuals will be provisionally treated as prisoners of war, but in assembly centres or prisoners' camps they will be separated from prisoners of purely Polish nationality. This applies to other members of minorities who report to the troops or are brought in by, for instance, the secret military police until the examination to which they will be submitted in the prisoners' camps gives appreciable results. If the members of the minorities bring arms with them, these will be collected by the troops and transferred by degrees to the camps and munition parks.

b) Minority representatives who are fighting for the Wehrmacht or are assigned tasks by them will report:

   1) In uniform and with the regular Polish equipment. They will abandon the Polish fighting units as a group, or will escape individually, and will make themselves known.
   2) As civilians. Means of recognition (see paragraph 4 of instructions).
   3) As parachutists in greenish grey-brown coloured overalls with a grenade, or also in civilian clothing. They are armed and furnished with explosive materials.

The minority representatives who are fighting for us (see par. 4) must be handled separately and conducted before elements belonging to Ic/V.O. of the Grenz-Schutz, section Kdcs. The arms and other weapons of struggle carried by these men will be taken and collected separately.

8.) It must be borne in mind that the Poles, who are famous for their cruelty and astuteness, will trick the German troops by adopting measures which are applied by men of German race.

9.) All those who form part of the army must be informed that in many places it will enter areas which are purely German or where the German population predominates. They should behave accordingly.

It will depend on the manner in which every man conducts himself whether the population of German race welcome joyfully the restoration of all the German areas to the Great German Reich.

Certified copy.
(Signed, PRINCE REUSS, Major.)

APPENDIX TWO - NOTES MADE BY M. R. CHAULET, FRENCH CONSUL, ON THE GERMAN MINORITY'S ILLEGAL ACTIVITIES IN POLAND AT THE BEGINNING OF THE WAR[128]

IN the light of the events which have occurred in Poland since September 1, certain facts which came to notice in Pomorze before that date deserve attention, since they quite clearly show that the German minority living in that province were thenceforth determined, if not thoroughly prepared, to play an active part in the event of an armed conflict between Poland and Germany.

The most salient of these facts would appear to be the following:

(a) *The numerical importance of the personnel of the German Consulate General at Toruń.*

Well-informed Polish circles declared that this Consulate General had some fifty agents. Certain of them travelled about a great deal and maintained close relations with the minority circles in Pomorze.

(b) *The tendentious articles of the Deutsche Rundschau.*

It was said that this daily, the organ of the German minority in Poland, and published at Bydgoszcz, was largely subsidized by the German Embassy. It participated in the life of the German minorities in Poland, and violently defended their cause. Certain of its articles appeared to be so clearly provocative in character that one was justified in asking whether they did not emanate from the Press bureaux at Wilhelmstrasse or from the German Embassy at Warsaw. The *starosta* (county administrative head) of Bydgoszcz often called the paper's director to order, and entire editions were confiscated. It may be of interest to note that the same articles were sometimes to be found in the Danzig dailies, after brief intervals and with small alterations.

---

[128] This document was handed to the Polish Government at Angers by the French Embassy to Poland, in April, 1940.

(c) *The activity of certain minority groups.*

Very varied groups and organizations (*Jungdeutsche Partei, Deutsche Vereinigung, Jugendherbergen,* agricultural co-operative societies, etc.) held frequent meetings, during which influential members (the Senator Hasbach was one) addressed the gathering. One may expect that not all the demonstrations of these societies were reported to the authorities, and that the members maintained secret relations among themselves.

(d) *A collation of varied but very characteristic incidents.*

During the three months prior to hostilities there was talk of the arrest of two German spies, talking Polish "like natives," close to Wejherowo and Tczew; of the discovery of arms (rifles, grenades, and even, it was sometimes said, machine-guns) in farms and houses belonging to German minorities, especially at Grudziądz, Starogard, Tczew, Bydgoszcz, and in a locality near Toruń, probably Grębocin. A sensational discovery of this kind was also made at Gniezno, near Poznań. For various reasons the local Press gave very little publicity to the results of the searches, which, however, sometimes came to light, and occasionally it was possible to obtain official confirmation in the course of conversation.

On September 1 at 5.30 a.m. the town of Gdynia was warned of the opening of hostilities by three German aeroplanes, which about six o'clock dropped bombs on the military port and on certain semi-military objectives. After they had gone the sounds of a fusillade of shots and the rattle of machine-guns were distinctly heard. The Consulate porter, who had been called out the previous evening by the A.R.P. service for a practice test and had been in the street all night, told me that the sound of firing came from Orłowo (a place about three kilometres from Gdynia and almost the same distance from the Polish-Danzig frontier). As the Polish troops were on the spot (they had a barracks at Orłowo) it seemed improbable that the German elements could have advanced so rapidly. It was learnt a little later that a Protestant pastor belonging to the German minority and fifty men armed with rifles, grenades, and even a machine-gun, had engaged the Polish troops stationed at Orłowo in combat. They thus occupied the bulk of the forces while, profiting from the confusion caused by this unexpected attack, the Danzig troops attacked from their side, and reached the outskirts of Orłowo, after breaking through the lightly held line of troops covering the frontier zone. The truth of this story was confirmed by what followed. Before leaving, about five in the afternoon, I learned that the pastor had been taken prisoner, had been given a warm time by the colonel, and that he would certainly be shot, if he had not been shot already.

When I tried to send a telegram about 8 a.m. the person to whom I entrusted it was informed that telegraphic communication with the rest of Poland was no longer possible. A little later there was a rumour that members of the German minority had been arrested for cutting the telegraph wires. One fact was certain: the French Embassy (at Warsaw) had been able to get the telephone number of the Consulate at Gdynia at 8.45 a.m., but it was not possible to make contact after that.

In the course of the day I learned that the first aeroplanes to bomb Gdynia had come from destroying the military hydroplane base at Puck. In this connection the rumour spread that in this locality an individual had been arrested making signals to the enemy airmen. Unfortunately I was not able to verify the truth of this statement.

During the journey from Gdynia to Warsaw, which I made by car, leaving Gdynia at 5.30 p.m. on September and arriving at the Warsaw Embassy at 2 a.m. on September 4, a number of illegal activities were brought to my knowledge.

After leaving the environs of Tuchola, which it was impossible to enter, I travelled on the road with the troops making a fighting retreat and coming from Chojnice. As there was a serious block of vehicles, I got out to find out what was happening, and so had an opportunity of exchanging some remarks with an officer. After telling me that a German armoured train had tried to penetrate into Chojnice and had been blown up, he made a reference to the attitude of certain minority Germans who had barricaded themselves in their farms and had fired on the Polish troops.

At Świecie in the morning of September 2, I heard from private persons that veritable battles had broken out the previous evening at Bydgoszcz and its environs between Polish troops and groups of minority

Germans, and that at Grudziądz members of that minority had been arrested for "communicating with the enemy." In the police headquarters of the same locality I saw three civilians brought in by two soldiers with fixed bayonets. I asked the reason for their arrest, and was told that they were minority Germans accused of furnishing information to the enemy. Under their arms they carried small document cases of black moleskin, both exactly alike. The chief of police told me indignantly that he had seen so many of them brought in since the previous evening that he was seriously beginning to ask himself whether everyone he spoke to was not a dangerous minority German in disguise who ought to be arrested.

At Chełmno, a town on the right bank of the Vistula and opposite Świecie, I saw ten of these individuals brought in to the *starosta*; three or four of them were carrying document cases of black moleskin. Once more they were minority Germans of the district who had been caught cutting telephone or telegraph wires or making signals to German aeroplanes, which flew over the district in groups and at such frequent intervals that there were not less than three air raid warnings in an hour and a half. While a search was being carried out at the houses of some of these minority Germans, detailed plans of the country had been discovered.

The *starosta* of Chełmno told me that a German aeroplane had been forced down at Toruń, and that its observer had been recognized as a "minority man" who had gone to Germany some months before to do military service. He believed that the same thing had occurred at Bydgoszcz, and he thought, apparently with good reason, that these two cases were not isolated. Naturally the roads which I had to take led at times past railway junctions, barracks, electric power stations, and farms occupying a strategic position. The German aeroplanes seemed to manoeuvre as though they were above a country which they knew well, and dropped their high explosives or incendiary bombs upon objectives so precisely that it is reasonable to suppose that the pilots knew the country or possessed very detailed maps.

During the night of September 2 to 3 my car was rescued from a breakdown by the owner of a large farm in the environs of Lipno. He invited me to go and rest for a while at his farm. He told me that in the morning of September he had caught a minority German who lived in the area just as the man was trying to cut telephone wires, and that he had handed him over to the military authorities. So that individuals belonging to the German minority were not merely pursuing their malevolent tasks only in the zone of military operations. It is true that the German airmen turned even areas far removed from the front into scenes of destruction.

Obviously I was not personally able to verify the majority of the facts cited above, but they have been related to me by people worthy of trust, who had sometimes been eyewitnesses. They may quite justly be regarded as the logical end and realization of the preparatory activity of "the times of peace."

R. CHAULET.

WARSAW.
September 5, 1939.

---

[i] Mr. S. N. Deposition 67.

Made in United States
Cleveland, OH
06 April 2025